The Healing Power
of the Past

Children seldom or never dare to live a happier or more fulfilled life than their parents. Unconsciously they remain loyal to an unspoken family tradition, which has hidden effects. As a result, children repeat certain behaviors and experience a fate similar to that of their parents. This burdensome inheritance has an effect even when family members appear alienated or adult children distance themselves from their parents. This revolutionary application of systemic therapy has found a way, through the use of Family Constellations, to discover underlying consequential family bonds and forces. This process reveals, in a visible way, that certain problems have their roots in the unfortunate inheritance of feelings, beliefs and life-principles, which have been carried unconsciously through the generations.

The Healing Power of the Past

The Systemic Therapy of Bert Hellinger

Bertold Ulsamer

Underwood Books
Nevada City, California
2005

The Publisher thanks Tom Breyfogle, Sheila Saunders, and Marcie Neville who helped to make this English edition possible.

Note from the editor Sheila Saunders: This book has changed me. I thank Bertold for bringing his experience and insight so eloquently to this manuscript. With candor and a spirit of inquiry, he illuminates the essence of this mysterious work. I also thank both Bertold and Tim Underwood, the publisher, for allowing me a part in bringing this instructive, enlightening, transformative volume to the English-speaking public.

First Edition, ISBN 1-887424-99-7
ten 9 8 7 6 5 4 3 2 1

Ulsamer, Bertold, 1948-
[Ohne Wurzeln keine Flügel. English]
The healing power of the past : a new approach to healing family wounds / by Bertold Ulsamer ; foreword by Bert Hellinger.– 1st ed.
p. cm.
Includes bibliographical references.
ISBN-13: 978-1-887424-99-8 (softcover)
ISBN-10: 1-887424-99-7
1. Family psychotherapy. 2. Systemic therapy (Family therapy)
    3. Hellinger, Bert. I. Title.
RC488.5.U47313 2005
616.89'156–dc22
2005018746

THANKS

First and foremost, for the valuable and exciting conversations, her support and her patience—especially in those last stressful days before the deadline of this book—I would like to thank my wife Gabriele.

I would also like to thank my colleague Sneh Victoria Schabel, with whom I led my first family constellation seminars, for her many valuable ideas, examples and encouragement. For me, that was the most valuable type of learning experience.

I would also like to thank Sheila Saunders for her editing and final overview of this English translation. She did such a great job!

Finally, my thanks go out to Bert Hellinger, who developed family constellations in the form that they are described in this book. Family constellations have changed and enriched my life in ways that I never expected. Beyond that, I would also like to thank him for the time that he personally gave me for this book, in addition to the ideas that he contributed.

CONTENTS

Author's Foreword

Today people seem to be sprouting wings. There are no apparent barriers that science and technology cannot overcome. Yet war, fear and environmental catastrophe are multiplying. We have wings, but where are our roots?

The family is the ground in which we take root. If we deny, discount or overlook these roots, the wings that we grow will be weak. Family constellation work is a way to discover these roots and to free them from that which weakens or binds them. Only then can the strength of the roots flow into the wings. Bert Hellinger, who developed the Family Constellation in the form presented, summed up his experience in this matter:

> "When the family is brought into order, an individual from that family can leave the nest. He feels the power of the family behind him. Only when the connection to the family is recognized and the responsibilities are taken up by the appropriate members, does the individual feel free of burden. Each can go his own way, without the past burdening him and tying him down."

INTRODUCTION

I congratulate the publisher for making Bertold Ulsamer's international bestseller, "Ohne Wurzeln Keine Flugel", (*The Healing Power of the Past*) available to the American public. It is a book that helps to explain why we often encounter difficulties in relationships even when all concerned are of good will. And it offers surprisingly simple solutions to such difficulties.

Bert Hellinger

To my father and mother

The Healing Power
of the Past

ONE

The Basic Elements of the Family Constellation

During a "family constellation", the hidden tensions, conflicts and influential relationships existing within a family become visible. The facilitating therapist works with these dynamics and often solutions can be found. Family constellations are surprising in form, process and effect.

This chapter covers the basic and essential aspects of family constellations in order that the following chapters, which present family constellations in detail, may be understandable to those with no previous knowledge of the material.

"Setting up" families is not a new technique, but Bert Hellinger developed this therapeutic method into something new. Using his approach, when the family of the person in question is "set up" (i.e. recreated using stand-ins to represent various relatives), previously hidden relationships come alive and are made visible. With experience, the family relationships and previously unrecognized ties across several generations can then be comprehended in a glance. A family constellation can be seen as a living family tree.

An Overview of
Family Constellations in Practice

A family constellation is best conducted in a seminar setting. Family constellations can also be done in a one-to-one session, but a workshop setting, using representatives for the family members is preferable, because this will produce a more complete impression of the family. In a workshop, participants come to look at family situations, their own or others. To do this work, participants do not need their own family members to be present. However, siblings, couples or a parent and child sometimes come and participate together and this can be an especially enriching experience for everyone involved.

The person who wishes to set up his family must have an "issue" to address—a specific problem to start with. For example, perhaps a grown daughter repeatedly feels angry towards her mother for no specific reason. In the family constellation, she looks for the unknown cause of her anger in hopes that through the workings of the constellation, her anger will shift, lessen or even resolve completely.

To begin, the therapist or facilitator (these terms will from here on be used interchangeably) asks the client about important events which have occurred in the family in the last two generations. The therapist does not inquire beyond the presenting issue and critical events in the family's history. The client then chooses (from among the workshop participants) persons to represent some of the living and dead members of his immediate family—parents, siblings, grandparents, aunts/uncles, or closely associated significant others (those determined by the facilitator to be immediately relevant to his issue), as well as a representative for himself. Generally speaking, men are chosen to represent the male relatives and women are chosen to represent the female relatives, although if numbers do not allow, a family member may be represented by a person of the opposite gender.

Now the constellation can be "set up". The space used for the constellation may be in the center of a group sitting in a circle or perhaps on a stage or area at the front of the room. The client spontaneously places each representative in the space, in relation to the other representatives, facing each in a specific direction. The client sets up his or her mother, father, etc., until the various family members have been positioned. The client places the representatives silently, without comment or explanation. It is important during this initial procedure that the client pay attention to his inner feelings, placing the representatives according to how he *feels* at that moment, without *thinking* about it, as the placement of the representatives is of great significance.

After the client has set up the family members who are deemed relevant to his issue, he* sits down in a seat from which he can easily observe the representatives. Then the constellation begins. Although the client may remain only an observer of what follows, he allows the words and actions of the therapist and representatives to affect him.

An amazing—and mysterious—phenomenon then takes place: the representatives are able to access the feelings and dynamic relationships of the family in question. They spontaneously experience relevant emotional affect. For example, if

*As a matter of custom and convenience, this narrative will frequently use the masculine pronoun without intending sexual preference or hierarchy.

a child or parent is set up near the edge of the designated area facing away from the others, this representative may feel disconnected and burdened. That can be interpreted as a situational reaction. But beyond such rational explanations, the representatives invariably experience many feelings, dynamics and connections existing in the family's past or present which are not otherwise apparent or visible. The representatives frequently feel novel physical sensations—their knees may shake, they may sway from side to side, their shoulders may become tense, they may experience stomach cramps. The representatives, in their respective roles, feel attractions and aversions toward the others in the constellation. They can point out those with whom they are angry and those with whom they would gladly have more contact. The roles within the constellation assume independent power and identity to the extent that anyone else, who at another time might represent that particular family member, will spontaneously react in a similar manner. A representative may even adopt a physical posture or repeat sentences frequently used by the family member they are representing.

At the onset of the constellation, the therapist begins by asking the representatives how they are feeling in their respective positions. After the feelings and relationships between the parents and children have first been checked out and expressed aloud, the therapist often suggests that the client set up other family members from past generations or the therapist may set up these additional members. Often, surprising things happen when family members who have long since passed away and been forgotten or were hardly known about are included by representation.

For example, a nephew can suddenly, almost magically, feel drawn toward the uncle who died many years ago in war.

The Basic Elements of the Family Constellation

Family constellation work has demonstrated that a clien
feels an inner (unconscious) connection to another fa..ily
member or ancestor will often have similar feelings toward
life and live out a similar fate. Indeed, one of the most meaningful of Bert Hellinger's discoveries is that children "take on"
the feelings and behaviors of older family members. They
may hold on to these feelings and behaviors—which are not
actually their own—for an entire lifetime. Bert Hellinger has
termed this phenomenon an "entanglement." Affected children are often "entangled" well into adulthood with one
ancestor or another. Depression, feelings of guilt, thoughts of
or attempted suicide and other psychological disturbances,
can often be traced to these hidden connections with other
family members. As long as a person does not recognize that
he is entangled, his feelings and behaviors will often be misunderstood, as well as influenced—even controlled—by
these invisible bonds.

One cause of "entanglements" occurs when a family
member has been shut out, or excluded and forgotten by the
family. Such family members will often be represented in the
next generation, or the generation after that. For example, a
father had an older sister who died in a traffic accident when
she was four years old. The death of this sister was so hard
on the parents and the other siblings, it shocked all of them
so deeply, that they rarely spoke of her. Thereafter, she
seemed almost forgotten.

To find out what kind of an influence this dead sister has
on the surviving family members, one need only set up a
family constellation and choose a representative for that sister.
In the constellation, representatives of the dead perceive and
feel as if they were living; there is no noticeable difference
between the living and the dead.

If the client has a connection to the deceased, the client's representative in the constellation will react immediately. He may for example feel sympathy or angst of some kind, when the dead sister is set up. The representatives of the other family members may react in some way as well. In the family set up, feelings and sensations change when representatives are added or removed, or when positions are changed. One person suddenly becomes fearful, another is relieved and so on. By observing these reactions, a client can determine with whom he is connected and possibly entangled and from whom he may have taken on feelings or burdens.

These encounters with the deceased in family constellations are often a step towards solution. If the deceased are honored, they become friendlier towards the living and their relationship with other deceased family members may change as well. Where previously a forgotten, deceased family member stood as a dark, threatening force in the background, he or she can now become a source of strength and support for the living.

The representatives' encounters with one another in the constellation occur under the therapist's guidance. After the client has set up all of the representatives, the therapist takes over, assuming the role of "director" during the entire family constellation.

The therapist first asks the representatives how they feel and what they perceive in their respective places. Often he proposes that they repeat simple sentences. Some of these declarations are intended to reveal tensions— e.g., "I am angry with you." Other statements relieve tensions or can heal damaged relationships and foster acceptance. Often a simple "I honor you," is enough to facilitate change.

Such a declaration will relieve tension only when it is accurate. The representative has a very fine sense of whether or not a statement is accurate and corresponds to what he is feeling. A representative may repeat the therapist's suggested statement, such as "I honor you," to another representative in the constellation and then when asked "Is it true?" may respond that the statement was not accurate. If he bows to honor the other representative, one can often tell by the look on his face if this gesture fits and is in earnest. The other representatives can also feel whether or not the statement fits and is accurate and true. If not they will reject it.

Appropriate statements have a positive effect. For example, one of the representatives may suddenly exhale and visibly relax. He or she may smile and stand up straighter. These responses are important. The more experienced and sensitive the therapist, the more frequently he or she can formulate accurate or applicable statements for the representatives the first time around and there will be less subsequent contradiction.

In a constellation, the place where a representative stands in relation to the other family members represented, has a significant effect on the feelings experienced. When the parents and children of a family are positioned widely apart, facing many directions, the chaos will be apparent and no one will feel right in his place.

However, when positioned or repositioned (by the therapist) in "good" order, every family member feels best in his or her place. Often, a good family order is represented in a constellation when parents and children stand facing one other. The father and the mother are turned slightly toward each other, so that they can see each other and their children at the same time, the mother to the father's left. The children stand in a half-circle facing the parents, in clockwise order according to age—oldest to youngest. When forgotten or excluded family members are given their respective place—either behind or at the side of the parents—it has a particularly healing effect. As a rule, every person is visible to the others, clarifying that each member has a place and belongs to the family system.

At the end of the family constellation, the client whose family has been set up takes the place of his representative in the constellation. In our example, the client who was angry with her mother would take the place of her representative. Until this moment, she has been observing her family from outside of the constellation. When she takes the place of her representative, she can consciously perceive this "new" family order and incorporate it into her image of her family.

A family constellation generally lasts between fifteen minutes and one hour, though they are sometimes longer or shorter. The goal is not to discover the myriad of possible relations that exist within a family, but rather to portray the strongest entanglements in which one is trapped and which stifle one's energy. A family constellation helps make these entanglements especially clear. Often, when these entanglements are recognized and relieved, a good order, in which everyone feels well, will manifest. This provides a natural conclusion to the constellation.

However, if a particularly explosive emotional situation is uncovered in the family, the therapist may terminate the constellation, to prevent further work from covering the situation back up. Sometimes a constellation is aborted when it seems to be "stuck" and the attention span and energy level of those who are taking part has been exhausted. However, these constellations, too, can stimulate change, move the client in the right direction and have a positive effect.

Family History

Facts about the family history are essential to family constellations. Family constellations need facts as a base. Researching one's family by asking parents, aunts, uncles, grandparents, even siblings and cousins about important family events, is appropriate preparation before setting up your own family. This is because events that occur within a family have a strong effect, which is visible across generations. The most important facts to ascertain are as follows:

- Did someone in the family die very young, in childbirth, in battle or by suicide?

- Did someone in the family commit a crime or are there other reasons for strong feelings of guilt in the family?

- Did the parents have previous marriages, engagements, partners or love relationships?

- Were there family members whose difficult fates made them "outsiders"—e.g., were they handicapped, financially embarrassed, immigrants, homosexual, born out of wedlock, seriously ill, unmarried, imprisoned or institutionalized due to mental illness?

- Has any child's relationship to his/her natural parents been severely impacted in some way (e.g., was a child adopted, raised by foster parents, separated from the parents at an early age or stillborn?)

- Was anyone forced to leave his home or homeland?

- Did anyone in the family have parents of two nationalities?

For instance, a family may have a forgotten great-uncle who was under psychiatric care, an aunt who was mentally retarded and died young or a grandfather who drank or gambled away his fortune. There will consequently be one or more children in the family for whom these relatives and their fates will have special meaning—even if these children never knew them or of them. When certain events or family members are treated as "family secrets," the stronger and more damaging are the effects.

Since past situations and events have an impact on the children, grandchildren and great-grandchildren in a family, when someone has thoroughly researched his family history the facts can be used very precisely in the family constellations. Sometimes parents find it hard to tell their offspring about clandestine or embarrassing family matters. It seems to be true that if one is truly ready to hear about a family secret, he will often be able to uncover the necessary information.

Sometimes a constellation is ended early when it becomes clear by the actions of the representatives that there are family secrets or important unknown facts about the family. If the client is able to find out the unknown information, a subsequent constellation may be brought to a complete conclusion with this newfound knowledge.

The Family of Origin System, the Current System and the Client's Problem

There are two different directions in which to explore a family with the help of a constellation—the past and the present.

To explore the past, one sets up the family of origin. The people belonging to this family are the brothers and sisters of the client, the parents and grandparents, the parents' siblings (the aunts and uncles) as well as the great-grandparents and so on.

Also belonging here are those who "made room" for the people in this system—people who left, for any reason, and therefore allowed others to enter the system. For example, a great-grandfather had a first wife who died early. He then married and his second wife became the great-grandmother. In this work, the first wife still belongs to the family system because she "made room" for the second marriage and the subsequent children, neither of whom would otherwise exist. Or perhaps a mother divorced her first husband and married another man, who fathered their child. The first husband would also belong to this family system. From all the possible members who could be represented in the constellation, the therapist decides who are the most relevant and starts with them.

One who wishes to examine his own present life would set up his current family system. In this case, the client is represented, as well as his or her husband or wife (or other partner in a love relationship) and the children. All previous partners of each parent also belong in this system, as well as any children from these previous relationships. Finally, all aborted children belong to this system as well. Again, the therapist decides who shall be set up to start off.

The "issue" is the question, topic or reason that one wants to undertake a family constellation. Whether the family system to be set up will be current or ancestral depends primarily on the nature of this issue.

Some issues are directly related to the family of origin, and these suggest an ancestral set-up, such as "I always had problems with my father," or "I have a very tense relationship with my sister." Or perhaps someone has been burdened by a particularly tortuous feeling, without knowing the source, such as, "I always feel guilty," or "I've felt sad and depressed for years," or "I've been lonely my whole life," or "I can't seem to find my place in life and I don't feel a part of my family."

The current system should be set up when the problem stems from events and relationships experienced in the person's own life—problems such as "The relationship with the love of my life fell apart and since then, I have no luck in relationships." Sometimes a couple comes to a seminar with an issue such as "We don't know if we should break up or stay together," or "Our child has trouble in school because he is nervous and hyperactive."

Finally, some problems are rooted in both systems. There are influences derived from the ancestral family added to current life experiences for which the person himself is responsible. For example: "I always have bad luck in my relationships with women. They never last more than two or three years." If a man always has bad luck with women, then the cause of this presumably lies in the ancestral system. On the other hand, it is worth noting, that if the man is over forty years old, he likely has numerous relationships behind him. Before a new relationship can be successful, he has to deal with his past, with the "skeletons in his closet." It is almost certain that he played some part in ending his previous relationships and that he himself contributed to the failure of these relationships in some way. It is necessary for a person to examine and come to terms with his own history. Otherwise he will continue to carry all of the unresolved problems with him, which diminishes his chances of becoming involved in a fulfilled relationship.

We are closest to the present—it is what most concerns and affects us. The nearer an event is to us in time, the more strongly it affects us. The further away, the weaker its effect. In that sense, the death of a sibling has a stronger effect on us than the death of a sibling of our parents.

Sometimes it is easier and more comfortable for us to examine the past, to focus on the behavior and responsibilities of others, namely, our parents and our ancestors. It can be uncomfortable and awkward when we set up the events of our own lives, because it is here where we must come face to face with our own behavior and accept the consequences of our choices.

Where children are concerned, it makes sense to start with the present. Children help "carry" the parents unsolved problems and burdens. When the parents see this dynamic operating in a family constellation, they often find the strength to face the past and deal with the burdens of their family of origin.

It is possible that the family of origin system and current family system will overlap in a family constellation. For example, sometimes the current system will be expanded in that the father or mother is placed behind the client. Or a client's family of origin system is initially set up and then during the final stages, the child of the client is set up.

To get a complete picture of the relationships in the family, a client may set up both systems over time. It is usually a good idea to let some time pass between the two constellations. This allows for the integration of the new information, image or resolution into one's life.

Some seminar participants, despite much lengthy description, cannot articulate a clear issue. In such cases it is good to postpone setting up a family constellation. The more clearly the problem is articulated and the more pressing the concern, the clearer will be the perceptions of the representatives in the constellation. An unclear articulation of the issue will cause the representatives perceptions to be vague and imprecise. . . . Clients with a serious issue who are ready to confront what the family constellation discloses, invariably experience a more revealing constellation. A serious issue can be recognized by its simple and concrete formulation. It can often be expressed in one sentence.

During my work with constellations I have encountered clients who have attended seminars in the past, who come again and formulate their issue in very general terms, such as "I always feel blocked and I want to release my creativity. Those instances when I gave in and went ahead with the constellation after being presented with a vaguely defined issue were always disappointing for the client. The usual result was a "harmless" constellation with few difficulties, in which the parents and children came quickly to a good ending order, but for the client, such constellations are frustrating. They may respond by saying, "There was more tension and lots of problems in my family—this constellation doesn't help me."

In addition, when a client is experiencing a lot of anxiety at the beginning of the seminar and is eager to get their constellation over with as soon as possible, it is a good idea to wait. This eagerness seems to inhibit the constellation's pace and depth, as well as clouding the client's real issue. Participants do not necessarily need to know exactly what they want out of the constellation for the constellation to be helpful. Every constellation has, to some extent, a beneficial and clearing effect on everyone who sees it. Sometimes the presenting problem changes during the course of the seminar, indicating that something shifted as a result of their observation of another's constellation, and something new has been brought to the foreground for them. Then, after two or three days of seminar work, the client finds more clarity with the problem he wants to address and is sufficiently centered to go about setting up the constellation.

On the other hand, some participants may feel that it is not yet time to carry out their own constellation. Then they experience something as a representative that results in insight related to their own situation. This may then bring resolution to their issue, even without seeing it addressed in their own constellation.

TWO

Children Help Carry the Burden: Discovering the Bonds within the Family of Origin

He who does not know the village from which
he comes will never find the village that he seeks.
—Chinese proverb

The family is a system in which certain laws and principles operate. Every family has a strong inner bond, regardless of how things may look on the outside and regardless of whether or not the family members feel or are aware of this inner bond. Likewise, children carry with them burdens and energies from their family.

This chapter describes the most important principles operating in the family of origin. Although these "laws" may result in much family unhappiness when unrecognized, if these orders are acknowledged and appreciated, they become a source of strength and inner peace. By working with family constellations, solutions can often be found which end ongoing discontent.

The Bond with the Family

All of us are deeply connected to our own families—to our parents, siblings and ancestors. This is not easy to recognize, because on the surface, things often appear to be very different. For example, even if someone separates from his or her family, he or she will still carry the family's burdens and energies. That person continues to be affected by the feelings, behaviors and fates of the family. The connections and similarities we have with our families go above and beyond our normal awareness.

> As Carmen started her first job seven years ago, she was happy that the job was 300 miles away from home. This was because Carmen had problems dealing with her family, especially with her mother. She called home once in a while out of a sense of duty, but these talks did not go well. It seemed that nothing had changed since her childhood!
>
> Once Carmen tried to tell her mother what she missed as a child. Her mother did not try to understand her and instead became angry. When Carmen came home for Christmas, arguments began on the first day and she always drove home feeling angry. The only person in her family with whom she got along and enjoyed talking to by phone was her sister.

At first glance, Carmen's situation seems to confirm that children are *not* connected firmly to their family. Hasn't she broken away and become free and independent? Carmen thinks that she cut herself free from her family and left the nest. She even promised herself she would never be like her mother!

Today, like Carmen, more and more children see themselves taking steps towards emancipation and independence from their parents. They cut themselves completely loose and start a new life far from home. Despite geographical distance, they still have connections to their family that are not merely emotional.

Family constellations demonstrate that we have a special, previously unconsidered bond, not unlike a biological connection, with all of the members of our family, living and dead. We usually suppose that only those relatives we knew, with whom we got along or had trouble, were important or had an influential effect on us. But, above and beyond those obvious situations, are invisible, imperceptible connections to other members of our families, *whether or not* we know or have even heard of them.

Carmen is connected to her siblings, parents, aunts and uncles, grandparents, etc., in that special way. The understanding that each and every one of these people "belongs" to the whole family as if it were an independent entity, is one result of the years of Bert Hellinger's work with family constellations. Every constellation tests and confirms these findings.

Hellinger's work with constellations has shown that a family is a system or an energy field in which certain orders operate. There are, with exceptions, regularly recurring laws that operate in this family field. One can compare a family, when looked at over many generations, to a mobile. If there is movement at any point on the mobile, there is a compensating reaction in a different part. Children are the family members most affected by this compensatory reaction. They unconsciously take over unresolved energies in the system so that the system as a whole can regain balance and order.

What is suppressed within a family does not disappear, but rather "floats" around within the system, awaiting an opportunity to emerge. These suppressions include unexpressed feelings, burdens of guilt and excluded family members. The newest family members, the children, feel this unexpressed energy, take it in and live it out, expressing it in their own lives. Children are thus "entangled" by their ancestors, as they take on their ancestors' behaviors, feelings and fates as their own.

Not all children are unconsciously connected to or entangled with their ancestors in the same manner. One child may be more connected to an aunt, another to an uncle and a third to a grandmother, all for different reasons. Boys are usually connected to male and girls to female family members. An "only child" may have a lot to carry if there were many difficulties in the family's past. Or perhaps there are only male children in the family with an aunt who has a difficult history. One of the boys would then become entangled with a woman, which can make him insecure about his own gender. The same can happen when a girl is entangled with a male ancestor.

These energies are an undercurrent influencing our behaviors, our feelings and our life's direction. Hellinger uses the word "soul" for this unconscious component that bonds us to one another. This family "soul" sees to it that the values, behaviors and fates of ancestors are remembered, resonating and manifesting in subsequent generations. Working with family constellations helps one become aware of hidden family influences and bonds between family members. Above and beyond this, one's own personal "soul" pushes one towards healing and resolution.

Let's take a look at how this shows up in Carmen's constellation.

The client places all of the representatives in relation to one another. Carmen* stands far away from her mother, but is facing her. In her life, Carmen feels rejection and a sense of distance from her mother. The mother has a cold attitude towards her daughter as well.

Her maternal grandmother died before Carmen was born, so they never knew each other. As the grandmother is "set up" the atmosphere in the constellation changes. The grandmother is positioned behind Carmen's mother. Good contact develops immediately between Carmen and her grandmother. They smile at each other and seem to care for each other. However, Carmen's mother is uncomfortable with her own mother behind her. As she turns around, she experiences a sense of rejection and distance towards *her* mother.

Having been told this by the representative, the therapist suggests that the mother turn to her daughter and say, "The relationship between you and me is like the relationship between me and *my* mother." The mother repeats this and Carmen listens intently. Suddenly Carmen smiles, having discovered a similarity to her mother and her mother's experience. The tensions between mother and daughter start to dissolve.

Further tensions are resolved when the grandmother says to Carmen's mother, "Through your daughter, I can love you, too." Then Carmen says to her mother, "Out of love for your mother, I love you as well." Now all three women look at each other in a friendlier manner and recognize how they are connected.

*In the descriptions of family constellations throughout this book, it is actually the *representatives* of the client and family members who are referred to, rather than the *actual* client/family members themselves.

Carmen's family constellation shows a dynamic between parents and children that is often revealed by this work. Every mother behaves in some way like her own mother. The mother's relationship to Carmen was neither warm nor loving. It was the same between Carmen's mother and *her* mother. Indeed, we can imagine this same pattern repeating itself over many additional generations. The grandmother was able to be loving towards her granddaughter Carmen, but not towards her own child. Love often flows freely between grandparents and grandchildren, while the generation in between feels little of this love. Indeed, rather than love, a parent may feel jealous of the relationship between grandparent and grandchild. What is unique to constellation work is the means of uncovering and resolving this common phenomenon.

Tensions in the family constellation are relieved when existing similarities and connections are acknowledged and spoken aloud, as in "Your relationship with me is like my relationship with my mother." These words, when expressed aloud, have an immediate and profound effect, not only on the emotional level, but also on the deeper "soul" level. Awareness of similarity replaces resentment and encourages compassion.

Acknowledgment also engenders goodwill. "Through your daughter, I can love you, too." The grandmother who loves her granddaughter is connected to her own daughter by that love. And the grandchild who loves her grandmother cannot entirely cut her own mother—the person who connects them—out of the picture. In this way, Carmen can rediscover the unfelt part of her love for her mother. Carmen had always been connected to her family in this deep way, even though she had distanced herself. In this she was similar to her mother.

Early Death

Every death in a family causes pain and sadness in the other family members. These feelings are sometimes so strong they seem unbearable. A family member who dies young has a particularly lasting effect on the whole family system. Note the next example:

> For years, Monica has suffered from bouts of depression, to the point that she considers suicide during those times when it is at its worst. Her depression apparently is affecting other members of the family. Recently her ten-year-old daughter, Catherine, has begun to suffer with the same problem.
>
> When Monica was asked, before her family constellation, if someone in her family had died young, it was confirmed that when she was three years old, her five-year-old brother died in an accident.

When someone dies young, that is before the age of twenty-five or so, this death has far-reaching, penetrating consequences for the rest of the family members. The family system is impacted beyond the normal feelings of grief and surviving family members are deprived of those individual and personal qualities unique to the deceased member.

In addition, the death has an immediate and profound impact on the surviving siblings as well. Feelings of survivor guilt arise. Deep inside, the survivors may feel it is unjust to live on, which may engender a hidden inclination towards death. Their desire to be with their sibling is best expressed by the statement, "I will follow you." This movement towards death in the siblings is unconscious.

A stillbirth has particularly grave consequences. Even a

stillborn child counts as a sibling. Every baby that would ordinarily live, even if born prematurely (i.e. starting with the fifth month after conception), belongs to the family system and its death has an effect on the others. A child born later does not need to know about its older, stillborn sibling in order to sense the death of the earlier child and carry a sense of guilt from being "allowed" to live.

If the father or the mother died when the child was younger than fifteen or so, the family constellation will reveal an unconscious movement towards death. Such movements may start at an early age, manifesting as accidents or reckless behavior and continuing into adulthood with suicidal thoughts or dangerous behaviors. "I will follow you, dear mother/dear father" would be an expression of the child's feelings.

A comparable feeling of guilt can also occur in adults. As is well known, this frequently happens to survivors of war or natural catastrophes, when most of the others involved have been killed.

The movie star Kirk Douglas illustrated such feelings when he became a religious man on February 13th, 1991, at age 75. He spoke about it afterward in an interview:

> "I wanted to fly from Fillmore to Los Angeles. Soon after take-off, our helicopter collided with a landing sport plane. We started to spin and we crashed on the runway from a height of about fifty feet. Two people died in burning kerosene, one of whom was just eighteen years old. Since then, I feel guilty to be alive. I have been to two psychiatrists, but they couldn't help me give my life meaning. I suddenly wanted more than to just entertain people in films. Since then, I know that God has a mission for me, which I am to fulfill."

From such guilt feelings, an inclination to die almost inevitably emerges, as well as the sentiment, "I will follow you."

From the outside, the observable effects seem to vary. When a person gets a disease at a young age, the cause is often that the will to live was weakened and the body reacted by getting sick. Some people move towards death through drugs and excess. Others live out the inclination to die by engaging in high-risk sports. In this way, race car fatalities may be caught in the wake of this phenomenon. This dynamic is also found behind a type of desperate energy or enormous pressure that drives a person to extremes, be it in athletics or in their career.

This yearning for death often leads people to the border between life and death. The fear of death, which inhibits others from living on the edge, does not seem to exist for these individuals.

This is illustrated by the story of Jacques Villeneuve, a Formula 1 race car driver. When he was a child, his father, who was also a race car driver, died in the ashes of his Ferrari. Recently, Jacques said in an interview:

> "When you race for the crown of motor sports, you sometimes feel, 'Whoa. That was close! I'm glad I made it.' It's like a ride on the razor's edge—you know that you almost went under. I don't have fear in a physical sense. There are moments when my heart starts to pound and it hurts deep inside. It is not fear, but it is a very unusual feeling."

With this understanding of the after effects of an early death in the family, one can see news events in a different light. A photographic essay on the anniversary of Elvis Presley's death declared, "One of the most financially successful artists of all time died a painful death—from too many drugs, endless fame, and an overdose of loneliness." A picture of two beds in his parent's house was captioned, "Two beds always stood beside each other in the parents' house—in memory of Elvis' twin brother, who died at birth." Dead at the age of forty two, weighing 275 pounds, Elvis' lifestyle can be seen as an expression of "I'll follow you."

Every early death leaves behind deep emotional wounds in the family. The inclination to die shows itself in Monica through depression and thoughts of suicide. The death of her brother had this effect, even though Monica was only three years old when her five-year-old brother died. Deep inside she holds the intention to follow her dead sibling. With a fine sense of perception, Monica's daughter Catherine has felt and reacted to her mother's moods unconsciously, even though her mother's brother died before Catherine's birth.

> When Monica's brother takes his place by Monica's side in the constellation*, Monica is at first afraid of him. The dead brother has no feelings for the little sister by his side. An important first step comes when Monica faces her brother, overcomes her fear and looks at him. Next, she bows to him and with that gives him her full attention. Then she says to her brother, "You are my older brother who died young. I honor you and your death. Please be happy for me, your little sister, when I live on."
>
> The big brother then looks at his little sister Monica in a friendlier way. Monica now has less fear of her brother and feels lovingly connected to him. The tremendous burden that had been pulling her towards death has suddenly shifted into a positive life force.

*Keep in mind that that these are *representative* of the family members.

The central facet of Monica's constellation is her encounter with her dead brother, who is "brought back to life" in the constellation. When Monica sees him and acknowledges his death, a certain distance emerges between the two of them. She discovers that he his own person with his own fate that she no longer has to follow. Her being able to differentiate between her fate and his, is further supported when she says to him, "Please be happy for me when I live on."

However, Monica's daughter, Catherine, had been in danger as well. The movement towards death that Monica had been feeling does not impact just her; it also affects the next generation. The children of those who carry the feeling, "I will follow you" (towards death), will sense and experience this disastrous pull towards death as well.

Family constellation work shows that children assume this urge to die. A magical belief arises, that they can actually fulfill the parents' fate *for* them. The conviction, "Better me than you," is born. The child would die in her parent's place!

The mother is sick and the child gets sick as well. Deep inside the child believes that if *she* becomes sick, it will relieve the mother of her sickness. The child imagines, "If I die, than she will be allowed to live."

This is exactly the case with Monica's daughter, who already shows signs of depression similar to those of her mother. The sentence "better me than you," is a clear expression of her desire to relieve her mother's pain and prevent her death.

> Monica's daughter Catherine is set up during Monica's constellation. She, in turn, feels lovingly connected to her mother's brother. Death is pulling on her as well.

Just like her mother, and at the suggestion of the facilitator, she bows with respect to her uncle and states, "You are my uncle who died young. I am your niece. I honor you and your death. Please be happy for me when I live on." The uncle and niece look at each other lovingly.

Ten-year old Catherine is not present during the actual constellation, although sometimes children are brought into the constellations of their own families—even as young as four or five. Nonetheless, it is a healing experience for Monica to witness her daughter's entanglement dissolving.

In family constellations one may notice a variety of behaviors showing a person being "pulled" towards death. Often a representative will stand looking into the distance, through a window or a door, and will feel pulled in that direction. When it is suggested that he take a few steps in that direction, something interesting happens—he feels more relaxed with each step. Likewise, family members relax as well, when someone departed distances himself from the family in this way. Sometimes, the children are positioned very tightly around the father or the mother because they want to stop that parent from leaving. In other words, they want to stop that parent from dying. In other instances, parents and children are found staring at the same place, as if at someone who should be standing there. Through questioning, it is learned that the first child was stillborn. His death was denied and at some point seemed forgotten. This first child is then set up in the constellation, in that place where everyone is looking and everyone in the family relaxes. The gap is filled. That which was denied is brought out into the open.

Hellinger discusses this essential component that leads to change:

When someone has an inclination to die in lieu of another, he should look into the eyes of that person. While looking into the eyes of that other person, he can say, "It is better that I die instead of you." If he really looks into that other person's eyes, he suddenly finds that this is not true, and cannot honestly be said. He realizes that it is not okay to die, because the other person loves him as well. That frees him from his blindness—but the love remains. In this way, blind love becomes enlightened love.

Feelings Which Have Been Taken Over

In the family system, children take on the feelings of other family members. Therefore, feelings that have been repressed in the family will be experienced and lived out by a later-born member. It is as if the strong inner bond between family members requires that every deep feeling finds expression.

> Robert is plagued by feelings of guilt, which emerge at the slightest incidents. He cannot escape these feelings. They overcome him without warning. In spite of all he does, he cannot seem to find a reason for these guilt feelings.

When someone is burdened by feelings that cannot be accounted for within his own life, it makes sense to ask *who* in the family would have the most reason to feel this way. Were there acts committed by or events experienced by a relative or ancestor that could or should have caused these feelings in them?

Robert researches his family history and discovers that his father left his first wife during the war and that she then died in despair. Afterwards, Robert's father married the woman who became Robert's mother. It seems the father had completely forgotten about his first wife.

If there was anyone in Robert's family who had a reason to feel guilty, it was Robert's father. This is confirmed by the constellation.

Robert* stands facing his father and mother and feels a connection with his father. The father's first wife, whom he left, is also set up in the constellation. Robert's knees suddenly start shaking, but the father looks on at his first wife, seemingly unfazed. Robert perceives a feeling of guilt towards the first wife.

So that the guilty feelings reach their "rightful owner," Robert stands in front of the father and says to him, "These are your feelings of guilt which I have been carrying for so long. Please take them back. It would be presumptuous of me to do it for you."

The therapist proposes that the father respond, "I take on my responsibility and my guilt and I carry it. You are just the child." After the father speaks these words, he suddenly starts to feel the guilt, but at the same time, he feels relieved and capable of assuming his responsibility. Robert feels himself freed of the guilt to the same extent that his father has taken it on and he experiences the guilty feelings flowing back to his father, the true owner.

*Reminder: it is the *representatives* of the actual family members who are referred to here.

The representatives can tell if such statements as, "These are your feelings of guilt which I have been carrying for so long," are accurate or not. Sometimes they experience a new feeling after such a statement, like a release or relief of an actual burden. Robert's representative can also sense whether or not the father is telling the truth when he says, "I take on my responsibility and my guilt and I carry it."

In constellations, feelings flow back to their rightful owners. An important thing in this regard is the client's inner picture of the family. When a child has taken over burdensome feelings from another family member, it can help to put a heavy object in the representative's arms, which symbolizes the feelings that belong to the other person. Later, the representative is asked to lay the object, slowly and deliberately, at the feet of the person to whom these feelings belong. When the giving back of these feelings is made visible in this way, one can see and feel how difficult it is to actually let go of this burden. Sometimes it takes a while for children to let go of the object.

Everyone has a duty in life to take responsibility for his or her own actions. When we are able to do that, we are rewarded with strength and dignity and we can shoulder the consequences of our actions. When Robert's father accepted his guilt, it "freed" him and enabled him to stand tall. His father's statement, "You are only the child," is not a judgment of Robert's worth, but rather it relieves Robert of his burden and corrects the order. The father assumes his own responsibility and the child is free of it.

Here is one more example: A client feels overcome by pain and sadness when there is hardly anything in her life that should cause her to feel like this. As she begins to think about whom in her family would have reason to feel this way, she remembers that her parents' first child was stillborn. This brother was never talked about. He seemed to have been completely forgotten. However, the pain and shock that parents experience when a child is stillborn is often unbearable. Rather than work through the pain, they lock their sadness inside. In this case, the daughter felt the repressed pain and was living it out in her own life.

This is how family traumas live on. Family constellations show us that in the long run, the impact of these hardships cannot be repressed. Children help carry the burden by taking over repressed feelings such as guilt, pain and anger and they experience these feelings throughout their life.

Crimes and Guilt

In families, a prevailing drive towards equilibrium and order ensures that injustice and maltreatment are atoned for. A serious offense such as abuse or murder, committed by a family member, can have a powerful, negative effect on the entire family, over many generations. Sometimes the consequences skip one generation and impact the next. The effects then reach far beyond the level shown in Robert's example above.

What is "guilt?" For me personally, before I came in contact with family constellations, the concept of guilt seemed archaic and questionable. "Guilt" to my ears sounded like traditional, outdated religious dogma—like confession and sin, fire and brimstone. Who can really see into the minds and hearts of others? Who can judge another's actions? Even the bible states, "Let he who is without sin throw the first stone." I went about my work in therapy with the attitude that every person does the best he can with what he has and that if one commits a transgression, an apology suffices. The concept of "guilt" seemed superfluous. However, my subsequent work with family constellations has shed new light on concepts such as "injustice" and "guilt."

Family constellations demonstrate an authority which directs individuals independently of mental justification and reasoning. When this authority finds one's actions to be unjust, it "ensures" that they are "paid" for. The representatives sense this guilt and experience a desire for atonement and reparation.

For example, when one person kills another—other than in self-defense—deep inside, the perpetrator perceives the injustice of his act, perceives himself as a murderer. For instance, family constellations show that soldiers who have killed other soldiers usually do not feel guilty of the act, on one level. That person's inner "authority" does not consider him a murderer. However, when that same soldier kills civilians, he counts as a murderer and will usually consider himself to be one.

Sometimes, such a perpetrator feels enormous guilt and later takes his own life. The biblical saying "an eye for an eye, a tooth for a tooth" seems to ring true, deep within us. Sometimes, however, the perpetrator lives on, unmoved. If a murderer refuses to take on his guilt, then the guilt lives on and finds expression through another family member. That can happen in two different ways: a family member in a future generation may become a murderer himself, or a family member in a future generation will identify with the victim(s) and in some way be pulled towards an early death—perhaps by committing suicide, or by living a life of atonement.

Jürgen became an alcoholic at a very young age. He routinely drank excessively and provoked fights. Even a prison sentence seemed to have no effect on him.

He never knew his father, because his father didn't return home after the Second World War. Practically by coincidence, he found out that his father was in the SS and had killed several Jewish residents of his city. After the war, he was never convicted of the crimes.

In the family constellations that I have done here in Germany, issues related to the Third Reich come up repeatedly. In constellation work the consequences of the Third Reich come to life before our eyes, because the perpetrators and the victims had children who carry on the effects of the past events. In almost every seminar, there is at least one participant like Jürgen, who has a relative that was somehow connected to a war crime. The constellations show that in such instances, the family has a long way to go before it can reach inner peace.

In Jürgen's constellation, the father is standing far away from the family. He is brought closer, looks at his wife and children and is prompted by the therapist to say, "I was in the SS and I killed Jews. I now take my responsibility and my guilt for this crime."

Jürgen's father states that the first sentence feels accurate, but the second sentence—in which he takes responsibility for his actions—felt mechanical and did not resonate with his feelings. Jürgen, his mother, and his siblings all feel tense and saddened in the father's presence.

When the therapist sends Jürgen's father out of the room, the family feels greatly relieved. The father is then brought back and reports that he felt better as well, when he was outside the door. He perceives that leaving the room was the "right" thing to do.

At the end, Jürgen turns to his father, bows and says, "You are my father. Through you I received the gift of life and that is the greatest gift there is. I thank you for it." He continues, "I give back your responsibility and guilt, and now I let you go." The father goes out the door and Jürgen feels as though a hundred-pound weight has been lifted from his shoulders. The father is brought in briefly once again and reports that he felt this to be the right solution. Then he leaves the room again.

A good note on which to end a family constellation is when the natural love between parents and children flows. Life flowed to the children through their parents and that is the most important thing. In the language of family constellations, that is "the greatest gift there is."

Jürgen owes his father thanks for giving him the gift of life, whether or not his father is a murderer. That is why the first step toward healing in the constellation is for Jürgen to express and feel this gratitude to his father: "You are my father, through whom I received my life. That is the greatest gift there is and I thank you for it." Love—or at least acknowledgement—is needed in order for Jürgen to be able to let go of his father. Returning responsibility and guilt to the rightful owner is possible only by honoring that person and their fate, which includes the consequences of their behavior.

Paying respect in this way is essential in order for children to become independent of their parents. If someone severs his relationship with his parents out of anger, the connection to them is suppressed yet strengthened. This invisible bond ensures an enduring connection and even though the parents may no longer feel connected, the child will.

One central principle demonstrated in family constellations is that every person must carry his or her own fate. That is, no one may assume another's fate or take responsibility for another's actions without paying a price in their own life. For children in the family, it is critical that each member take responsibility for his or her own actions.

Jürgen's father was a murderer. No one else can shoulder his responsibility. He must take on that responsibility himself and carry the consequences of his actions. Children are not entitled to, nor do they have the right to get involved, either by judging their parents or by taking on their parents' guilt. If they do, the effect of the traumatic event will be carried on. However, neither course of action alters the essential connection to the parents.

Why do all of the representatives taking part in Jürgen's family constellation feel a sense of relief when Jürgen's father leaves the room? Bert Hellinger discovered in his work with constellations, that between victim and perpetrator a new connection emerges that is stronger than the connection between the perpetrator and his own family. That is why the perpetrator must leave his family, and in this example, why Jürgen must let his father go. This is expressed by his sentence, "I leave you your responsibility and your guilt, and I let you go."

The father, too, feels that this is the right thing to do, which is why he feels better outside of the room. The enduring love of the perpetrator for his family resonates in that feeling. He knows that if he stays with his family, Jurgen and the other children are at risk for taking over his guilt. That's why it comes as a relief to him, as well, when he leaves his family.

Sometimes the perpetrator is unable to acknowledge the victims and the children or grandchildren of the perpetrator feel a connection to the victims, a connection which influences their lives. During the constellation they want to lie at the side of the victims and share their fate. However, that is not a good solution. A family constellation described in Bert Hellinger's book *Der Abschied* demonstrates a memorable example of this phenomenon:

> Repeatedly, the client had the feeling that she should die—that something was hovering over her that she could not grasp. During the constellation, she revealed that her father had committed suicide and that her grandfather had been a soldier in the SS and had murdered women and children.
>
> Hellinger set up ten people to represent the murdered children. A long, moving session resulted in the grandfather having to leave the room. The client still felt drawn to the sides of the dead children—so much so that Hellinger finally let her stand among them.
>
> *Hellinger to the client:* "How do you feel?"
>
> *The client:* "This is what I deserve. That is how it feels. It's a big a relief."
>
> *Hellinger to the dead Jewish children:* "How is it for you?"
>
> *1st Jewish child:* "I'm experiencing death as being something impersonal, as if the murderer has nothing to do with it and the grandchild has absolutely nothing to do with it. For me it doesn't seem appropriate for her to join us. She should go to her family. I am not interested in her atoning for this. That is not her job."
>
> *2nd Jewish child:* "I got weak in the knees when she came over to us. I felt that she didn't belong with us. . . ."
>
> *3rd Jewish child:* "It feels like it is too much."
>
> *4th Jewish child:* "I don't want her sacrifice. She doesn't owe that."

5th Jewish child: "To me, it is her duty to end the pain with *her* children."

The other five representatives of the Jewish children reacted in a similar way. The solution first came when the client looked the children in their eyes for a long time and then said, "Now I will stay (alive)."

When the client looks into they eyes of the murdered children, she starts dissolving the feeling of unity that she has with them. She begins to see herself as separate and is able to perceive her own fate, separate from that of the victims. At the same time, she recognizes that it is not appropriate for her to live as if she were one of the murdered children.

Similarly, it is sometimes seen that the children or grandchildren of a victim take on perpetrator energy. Descendants of victims and descendants of perpetrators are at risk for taking on the energy of either party in the crime. With family constellations, in both cases, children can be helped to see that they are separate from their ancestor and the entanglement may be resolved.

In cases in which the father or mother or both have committed such serious transgressions that they must leave the room, what does that really indicate? What effect should the family constellation have on the client's life, on his reality? Does it mean, for example that Jurgen is supposed to kick his elderly father out of the house?

It cannot be overstated that family constellations work on the client's inner picture of the family. The inner picture and the reality are two different things. Family constellations do not teach individuals how to deal with other people. They work on a much deeper level.

One of my seminar participants had to let [the representative for] her mother, leave the room. The constellation showed that her mother had abandoned her when she was a child and had therefore lost her rights as a mother. As an adult, the participant met her mother again and they began having regular contact. In a later seminar, the participant told me that she felt as though she could have contact with her mother in an open and uninhibited way, but the special connection that she had felt as a child towards her mother had disappeared.

Recent discoveries have shown something new in this regard. The connection between murderer and victim becomes clear when victims are set up in a constellation. They frequently show shock and angst at the sight of the murderer. The murderer on the other hand often has trouble looking the victim in the eye. One method discovered by Bert Hellinger, demonstrates the power of this new bond between perpetrator and victim: The victim lies on the floor as if dead and the perpetrator lies down beside him. Initially, a sense of tension pervades the room. After a while the tension subsides and at some point, there is peace. It is as if the differences between perpetrator and victim disappear after death. In time, all become equal. With this movement, the perpetrator can stay.

Here is an excerpt from a letter written to Bert Hellinger from a constellation participant:

> Since the last seminar, I have a completely new feeling towards my grandfather, who was imprisoned because of his Nazi activities and had to leave the room in the constellation. It was so good to see him lying with the victims. I was able to honor him so much more and to leave him in peace and my feelings are now so much more peaceful. And to be honest, I am able to let it go. When he went out the door, there still

remained a residue of guilt. The new view of my family has a completely different effect on me. This is surely also because I was a representative in another, similar constellation. That was very good for me, being able to bow to both the victims and the perpetrators.

Special "Fates"

One important facet of the inner bond of a family is that every member of a family "belongs" to that family in the same way. Every family member deserves attention and has their rightful place, equal to all the others. When any member is excluded from the family, this brings bad consequences for the next generation.

> Ingrid had never had the feeling of really belonging to her family. She always felt like an outsider. She moved out of the house when she was eighteen and got married at that time. The marriage did not last long, and her next relationship also fell apart quickly. For the last ten years, she has lived alone and has hardly any friends or acquaintances. The small bit of contact which she has with her parents and siblings is more of a burden.
>
> When she began doing family research, she found out that her grandmother had had a mentally retarded sister. In this well-to-do family, however, it was considered shameful to have a mentally retarded family member. Consequently, the sister was given away to a home at a young age. She died there after three years and no one in the family ever mentioned her again.

The fates of those who have been unjustly excluded from the family are repeated in subsequent generations. No member of a family can simply be forgotten. The inner authority of the family members—one could call it the "family conscience"—does not allow it. A person shut out of his or her family (as was Ingrid's great aunt), will be represented by a later-born family member, who takes on a similar fate. This is how an excluded person is brought back in to the family's awareness.

> In her constellation, Ingrid is at first standing at the periphery, far away from the other family members. She feels somewhat detached, as if she doesn't belong with the group. As her great aunt is set up in the constellation, Ingrid is suddenly changed. She beams at her great-aunt and wants to come closer to her. When she is finally allowed to stand at the side of her great aunt, she feels happy and satisfied.
>
> In the next step, she is positioned facing her great aunt, who says to her, "I was born retarded, put into an institution and died at a young age. It is my fate and I carry it." Ingrid bows deeply to her great aunt for a while and then says, "I honor you and your fate. You belong to our family. Please be happy for me if I belong to our family as well." The great aunt looks at her and says, "You can also have a bond with me even if you belong to the family." Ingrid feels relieved and freed.

Ingrid feels connected to her great aunt and in a way, represents her. She doesn't represent her completely, of course, because Ingrid is not retarded and does not live in an institution. However, to an observer, it seems as if she is trying to imitate the fate of her great aunt as she withdraws from her family and lives out the inner feeling of separation and loneliness. This happens without Ingrid's conscious intention. Ingrid did not even know of her great aunt. But even that does not matter. The powers that work within a family are compelling and in this case, they determined Ingrid's fate.

In this way the fates of those whose lives were forgotten or repressed by the family are reenacted. That could be, for example, someone sent to a psychiatric institution or to prison, or someone who was banished from home and subsequently emigrated.

Also, a nun or a monk who lives in a monastery or convent, or a priest, to a certain extent, has shut himself off from his family. The person in question takes a vow of celibacy and therefore will not have children. In this way, they shut themselves out of the cycle of life that flows from parents to children. He who devotes himself to heaven has decided against a normal life on earth. Family constellations often show that such decisions are made out of an unconscious sense of duty to an ancestor who was shut out of the family.

People from a later-born generation may follow their ancestors into an exclusive lifestyle. They leave their own family and live a life similar to their ancestor's. In this way, fates are repeated over generations and often go so far back that it cannot be determined which ancestor it started with.

Children Remain Loyal to Their Parents

Children are loyal to their parents—to their father and mother equally. Out of loyalty to their parents, they repeat similar fates and similar misfortunes. Children seldom if ever risk having a happier, more fulfilled life than that of their parents. This is because if a child were to have a happier life then his father or mother, in a sense it would feel, deep down, as if he were a traitor.

Thomas and Maria got to know each other as teenagers and fell in love. They have much in common and they understand each other almost without speaking. Both of them come from broken homes. "That's why we want to—and will be able to—do it better," they said, and they married at a young age.

After a few months, they experience their first big disappointment. Subsequently, they repeatedly hurt each other and do things which make the other unhappy. For a few years, they try to keep it together and even have two children. Finally, they give up and separate.

"What did we do wrong?" they ask each other. "Where did this inability to make each other happy come from?"

If one looks into the roots of the bonds between parents and children, one finds a deep love from the children toward the parents at the source. Children love their fathers and mothers unconditionally and are even ready to sacrifice their life for them. They remain deeply connected to their family and their parents forever. This connection is independent of who the child grows up with or the feelings they have toward certain family members (e.g., "I like my father, but not my mother"). This unconscious love is archaic. It shows itself in the magical and unconscious belief that they can relieve another person of his fate (e.g., "better me than you!"), or at least reduce its effects by sharing that fate. This love is naive and in a certain way, blind.

When a child lives out the same fate as his father or mother this love is "fulfilled". Thomas' and Maria's parents were unhappy, bitter and frustrated in their marriage. If Thomas and Maria were happy and satisfied, they would lose part of their connection to their parents. In their hearts that would feel like a betrayal and they therefore resist it.

Unhappiness and pain are passed on from generation to generation in this way. Being deeply connected, family members carry on pain and unhappiness from one generation to the next. Distancing ourselves from our family out of anger or rage only works on the surface. Deep inside, we are still connected and we live out the role that reflects that connection.

> Thomas sets up his family and it is shown that he feels much sympathy for his unhappy father. Thomas looks at his father and says, "I live just like you." Then he pauses for a second and adds, "Out of love." After he says this, tears well up in his eyes and he is suddenly aware of the extent of his love for and connection to his father.
>
> Then Thomas bows to his father and says, "I honor you and your fate and I leave it with you." He continues, "Please look kindly on me if I have a happy relationship." Now the father looks lovingly at Thomas and says, "I am happy if you have a fulfilling relationship."

Children see their parents' problems and say to themselves, "I will do things differently—I will do things better than they did!" A certain amount of disdain towards the parents is hidden in such sentences and the children appear superior to and more capable than their parents. Later, in middle age, the child must admit to an unmistakable similarity to the parents and the realization that despite previous intention, they were no more successful than their parents were.

When Thomas says to his father, "I live just like you— out of love," he brings his deepest love to the surface. This touches his heart and from this state, Thomas is able to honor his father and his father's life.

"Please look kindly on me if I have a good relationship."
It is as if he is asking the father for his blessing. In today's
world, this type of a request may seem strange. However, in
family constellations, we see the effects of this request for
Thomas. The father, too, feels that his fate has been acknowledged and honored, and he is pleased—relieved—if Thomas
has a good marriage.

The sentences which Thomas says during the constellation, although simple, bring a release. However, emotionally
it demands a lot to say these words and consequently, to
accept their meaning. If Thomas honors his father and leaves
his fate with him, the blind love of a child changes into a more
mature, enlightened form of love. Parents and children
remain connected by this love, which enables each one to
carry their own fate.

> A woman with cancer is brought in a wheelchair
> onto the stage where Hellinger is working. He asks
> about her condition. She smiles and says, "I have
> cancer."
> "You seem happy," Hellinger replies. "You smile
> when you talk about it." He then says to the audience,
> "When a person smiles when they talk about some-
> thing bad, it is a sign of a systemic entanglement—
> they are happy when the 'prescribed' fate is fulfilled."

A deep inner satisfaction emerges from the connection
with one's family. This silent happiness is revealed by the
slight smile that many people display when they talk about
their problem. People complain about their financial situation
or their unhappy marriage, with a smile on their face.

If you look for this small smile, you will see it often when
people talk about their problems. In these cases, advice and

offers of assistance have no effect, because they interfere with the secret pleasure one derives from fulfilling a fate.

Here is one more example of the influential but secret bonds within the family that I have seen in my work:

> Unexpected difficulties were encountered by a medical doctor. After much therapeutic consultation, she was able to a put her plans into action. She rented new office space for her practice, and wanted to devote herself completely to alternative medicine. Just before she was to open her practice, however, she had an emotional low and lost all confidence in herself.
>
> When she investigated career successes or failures in her family's history, she remembered a grandfather whom she loved very much. After the war, her grandfather was unable to get "back on his feet" career-wise, and had to do small-time acting around the country—something the family considered shameful.
>
> If this client were to enjoy success in her career, she would be, in a way, disloyal. I chose a representative for the grandfather and proposed that she bow to him, honor his fate, and request his blessing for success in her career. She did this solemnly.
>
> A few weeks later she told me that her "unexplainable" career block had dissolved.

In this way, we gain a fresh perspective in areas such as our abilities, strengths, mental blocks and financial capabilities. It is seen clearly how children complete familial "role assignments". A child who is "assigned" success in their career will do everything possible to achieve this—in the name of the family. On the other hand, loyalty to the family can also require that a person be *un*successful. In these cases, a person will sabotage their own chances for success.

This unconscious loyalty is very powerful. On the surface, the contact a child has with his family may seem limited or even hostile. But even these children are serving the family by completing a task which has been passed down from a previous generation. Everyone accepts without question what is demanded of them by the ordering principles of the hidden systemic dynamics.

This loyalty that children have to their parents has never been given sufficient attention in theory or in practice. Until now, psychologists and therapists have assumed that children, first and foremost, need the love of their parents. The focus has been on the assumption that children do everything they can to be loved.

Family constellations show that children themselves possess an enormous amount of love and love their parents "back" with equal intensity. Growth towards a more mature form of love is at the same time a step toward being more independent, which is not easy for a child. Gradually, the child disconnects himself from the formerly constrictive, seemingly inseparable connection, which, in spite of all its problems, gave him warmth and security. The child must now take on more responsibility for his life. But as the child moves away from his parents, he feels guilty, as though he is doing something wrong.

The strength to leave the parents' house arises in a child when he looks his parents in the eyes. Formerly, the relationship was more symbiotic and deep inside, the child did not feel much difference between himself and his parents. However, when the child looks deeply into the eyes of his father or mother, he discovers a person separate from himself. Above and beyond that, he recognizes that the person looking at him also loves him back. Parents want the best for their children. To them, it is not desirable when a child follows their path into the same problems and unhappiness or carries on their burdens.

The Interrupted "Reaching Out"

Although many entanglements arise from the ancestral system, not all of life's troubles come from that source. One noteworthy cause of problems, the interrupted "reaching out," was detailed by Bert Hellinger.

Every child feels the desire to "reach out" to his mother and father in order to find love, protection and security. If the child suffers an early separation from the parents or experiences major rejection or emotional injury by them, fulfillment of this desire is abruptly and harshly interrupted.

For example, let's say a child is admitted to a hospital for three months at the age of one and a half. The hospital is far away from home and the parents seldom visit. The child experiences an emotional shock from this separation. After that experience, the child no longer has enough trust to follow the spontaneous impulse to reach out to his mother and father. The natural "reaching out" has been interrupted. The strong yearning for the parents remains, but now this feeling turn into sadness and pain, anger and frustration. A person who has had this experience as a child, often finds it difficult to love completely as an adult. He gets stuck in the gap between the yearning and the negative feelings connected with the yearning. Often he unconsciously provokes the rejection which he secretly expects. He is plagued by sadness, pain, anger and frustration. He can take out his rage on a cushion for years in therapy sessions, without his anger changing in any essential way for the better. This is because the rage is a secondary feeling—the primary feeling is the longing to be close to others.

Fulfillment of this "reaching out" brings healing. Hellinger sits across from the client in such constellations and lets the client be carried back to the time when this separation shock occurred. Then he asks the client to hold out his or her hands and say "please." It is moving to see how difficult this can be for the person affected, as pain and disappointment run deep. When this request, this "please," is actually articulated, the therapist can, as a representative of the mother or father, take the client in his arms and hold him. With that, the "reaching out" which had been interrupted for so long, is completed. The desire reaches fulfillment. When that occurs, old negative feelings dissolve.

The Phenomenon of Bonds

Up to this point, I have described the many different types of inter-generational family bonds which Bert Hellinger experienced in his work. Today additional bonds have been discovered, as if a veil has been lifted on what was always there. These bonds go still deeper and how they function is not yet clear. We are just now beginning to discover their causes and effects.

In France, Anne Ancelin Schützenberger, a Professor emeritus of psychology at the University of Nice, researches unusual bonds and connections. She mainly researches how traumatic events affect families over generations. The following paragraphs are partially based on an article by Albrecht Mahr on Schützenberger's work. Schützenberger calls her work "psychogeneology," and has written a French bestseller about it, currently in its 11th printing, called *The Ancestor Syndrome*.

> The client, Barbara, came in for treatment because of panic attacks and nightmares about soldiers in helmets. After researching the past generations of her family, she found a connection to the war of 1870, between Prussia and France, where a horrible bloodbath claiming 25,000 lives occurred. She discovered that her great-grandfather, Jules, had fearfully observed the battle, hidden behind a tree with his grandfather. After the history of her family had been researched and discussed, her nightmares stopped. However, a certain amount of pain remained. Barbara researched further. Her first panic-attack happened on an August 4th. She found out that the battle of Wissembourg happened on the 4th of August, 1870, and that several of her family members were killed or wounded there.

One main facet of the work of Schützenberger, is the noticeable connection between ages or dates on which accidents or disasters occur in the family. For example, with one client, the fatal poison gas attacks in World War I, at Ypres and Verdun, France, played a role in her asthma.

> A client had a four-year-old daughter who suffered from asthma and repetitive nightmares since birth. She regularly woke up coughing and screaming in the night. The daughter was born on the 26th of April. Ms. Schützenberger immediately thought of the 1st World War, when on the 22nd of April, Germany attacked with poison gas for the first time. "Did you have family near Ypres or Verdun?" she

asked the client, who recalled that her grandfather's family lived near Ypres.

During their next meeting, the client happily informed her that something like a miracle happened. Since the last session, her daughter had had no more instances of waking up in the night with angst or asthma attacks. But last night, these symptoms had returned. Ms. Schützenberger suggested the child bring a drawing of her nightmare to the next session. The child exhibited the drawing and said, "This is a diver's mask with an elephant's trunk on it. That is the monster which tortured me every night." The drawing resembled a gas mask from World War I.

As the client researched the archives, she found out that her grandfather's brother had been gassed at Ypres and her great-grandfather wounded and decorated at Verdun in 1916. When these events were spoken about in the family, the child's nightmares ceased and a year later had not returned. April 26th, the child's birthday, was the date of the last gas attack on Ypres.

Another example:

After a successful operation for cancer of the larynx, a client suffers from a constricted throat and has difficulty breathing. Beyond that, she is very worried about her younger brother Francois, who almost suffocated from diphtheria at the age of six months and has since been handicapped.

It is discovered that her grandfather was present during the poison gas attacks at Verdun. After this discovery, her breathing condition improved. However, something odd remained. The client often puts her hand to her throat, wears a short red necklace, and has repeated cold chills. These all remind Ms. Schützenberger of the French Revolution.

The client does further research and finds, more or less by accident, a relevant family history. She is shocked to discover that five of her ancestors died under the guillotine. One, who died on Jan. 9th, 1793, was named Francois. Her own brother, also named Francois, was born on January 9th, 1963. With this knowledge, her breathing problems go away.

When we pay attention, we notice these odd coincidences more often. If we hear about only one such event, we can brush it off as happenstance. However, when we repeatedly discover such events, then the term "coincidence" seems doubtful. Even Bert Hellinger tells of a family in which three men of different generations during the last three hundred years committed suicide, on the 31st of December, all at the age of 27. Research showed that the first husband of the great-grandmother died on the 31st of December, at the age of 27. He had likely been poisoned by his wife and the man who became her second husband.

Here are a few more examples from Schützenberger:

A man, age 29, suffered a hang-gliding accident in the month of August. The accident left him paraplegic. His father was also left paraplegic in August, at the age of 29, after an accident in World War II, while he was a prison laborer in a foundry.

In 1993, the actor Brandon Lee died while working on the set of the movie *The Crow*, when a pistol that had mistakenly been loaded with real bullets, was fired at him. Exactly 20 years earlier, his father Bruce died in the same way, during the making of the film Jeu de La Mort.

President John F. Kennedy contributed to his own murder when he, despite warnings, rode in a convertible through a crowd on the 22nd of November. His great-grandfather Patrick also died (at age 35) on the 22nd of November.

Researching illnesses and traumatic events in your family's past is a worthwhile task. Schützenberger found that there are "periods of susceptibility," when we are in danger because of our unconscious need to balance out the fate of our ancestors.

Sometimes patients have a lot of angst or even panic before an operation. Spurred on by the findings above, it was found at the University Surgical Clinic at Brest in Sherbroke, Canada, that patients had an above-average tendency to schedule operations on the same date on which an ancestor had died. According to this study, when other, less emotionally-charged dates were chosen, the amount of anesthetic needed and the number of complications after the operation were reduced by 50%.

Thus we begin to get a glimpse of the perplexing ties and bonds that exist within a family. We will likely discover more and more hidden connections in this area as time goes on.

THREE

Love, Partnership and Children: Taking Responsibility for One's Own Life

Love is a smoke made with the fume of sighs;
Being purg'd, a fire sparkling in lover's eyes;
Being vex'd, a sea nourish'd with lovers' tears
What is it else? A madness most discreet,
A choking gall and a preserving sweet.
                    - Shakespeare, *Romeo and Juliet*

This chapter deals with the life of man and woman in a relationship. It is also about one's existence as the mother or father of a child. All of the important people in our life build a new system—the current family system. In this system, there are orders and principles which affect the flow of love. When these are not attended to, there are consequences, for oneself, ones's children and their children.

Love and Order—A Contradiction?

The essentials for happiness and fulfillment in a relationship seem to be crystal clear to everyone. "Love" is the answer. Good, but frequently the "love" found at the beginning of a relationship later disintegrates.

Why is this? During the day in and day out of a relationship, arguments and power struggles arise, leading to frustration, pain and disappointment. Many partnerships end in rationalization: "We were no longer meant for each other . . . ; We grew apart . . . ; We weren't right for each other from the start . . . ; Maybe, things will work with the next one."

So it seems that love alone is not enough. We also need healthy ways to relate to one another. A plethora of books on relationship in the bookstores tell us, "Be open and honest! Communicate! Resolve conflict immediately!" Is there something above and beyond such easy counsel? What does it mean, for instance, when Bert Hellinger uses the word "order" with regard to love? Order and love seem to represent opposite poles. They seem disruptive of each other rather then compatible. Doesn't "order" put feelings into compartments and build dams against the stormy flood of our feelings? Isn't modern life limited by the use of order?

Life is full of contradictions but since truth rarely belongs exclusively to one side, thinking in opposites, such as "right" or "wrong", does not bring solutions. Family constellations offer a new understanding of the contrasting dynamics of "love" and "order." A person who jumps into new relationships with complete abandon, who leaves everything behind with each new love, will end up just as unhappy as the insecure person who holds on to partnership too tightly. Both are missing genuine love. Real life is lived between the poles.

If "order" is a reasonable contrast to "love", then what type of order are we talking about? Surely not the kind of social order which sometimes forced our ancestors to live their entire lives in loveless or destructive marriages. That old social order has almost completely collapsed. In terms of social relationships, stability is disappearing and we live amidst insecurity. We get hurt, we hurt others and we carry "bravely" on.

Are there elements of the old, outdated orders that could be helpful? Some of those orders were structured around the basic rhythms of life and are therefore worth preserving. Men and women live on this earth as sexual beings. Their sexuality exists, in turn, for procreation. After basic survival, propagation of the species is the strongest human drive. To secure procreation, cultural codes and orders have been built around that drive.

With the use of family constellations, it is possible to see these orders operating at a very deep level. Family constellations expose hidden dynamics and structures of relationships. Basic themes in life are reflected in constellations in the form of movements—shifts and interactions—which may be observed over and over again.

One important basis for a healthy relationship is an equal exchange of giving and taking. When one partner gives something to the other, an imbalance is created in the relationship and there is a need in the giver for compensation. If the receiver gives something back, then this tension is resolved. If he gives back just a little bit more than he was given, it is the other partner's turn to reciprocate. With this give-and-take, a positive kind of tension is created within the relationship. Bert Hellinger explains it in the following way:

Happiness in a relationship depends on the balance—"balance" in the business sense—of give and take in the relationship. A small balance brings only a small profit. The bigger the balance, the deeper the happiness is. However, that has one big disadvantage—it is more binding. Anyone who wants freedom should only give and take a very small amount, this therefore allows only a little to flow back and forth.

However, one should also only give and take as much as the other is ready to accept and give back at the same level. If one person gives more than the partner is able to give back, then the partner feels antagonized or pressured and gives back even less, and the imbalance becomes steadily larger.

Relationships in which one only gives and the other only takes are bound to fail. At some point, one or the other can no longer stand the imbalance and will leave, because this disequilibrium creates a pressure that must be relieved. The person who leaves or ends the relationship may unexpectedly be the one who *received* too much.

Especially surprising are Hellinger's statements that what holds true with the balance of positive things also pertains to the balance of negative things. If one person does something hurtful to another, there emerges a need to make things even. The "guilty" one should make amends or "pay back" in a way that corresponds to the degree of damage. That helps the relationship. However, it is also good for a relationship, when the hurt party demands a smaller degree of compensation than truly fits the original transgression. Similarly, the hurt party can also respond by doing something *less* hurtful back.

A man or a woman who is too "good" to demand atonement, for example by immediately and completely forgiving the partner who hurt him or hurt her, damages the relationship at the deepest level. The guilty party loses the opportunity to atone and the need for this goes unresolved. With that, the disequilibrium becomes greater. The hurt partner is the victim, but at the same time, by quickly forgiving, he is "above" the perpetrator. Then he comes across as the better person, which is not necessarily so.

Man and Woman in Relationship

In a relationship, masculine and feminine energies meet. The masculine energy is passed to the man through his father and forefathers. The feminine energy is passed to the woman through her mother, her grandmother and so on. If the relationship between father and son or between mother and daughter is damaged, the ability to connect or relate to the corresponding ancestors is also interrupted.

> Marie is unlucky in love. She has an easy time getting to know men and starting a relationship, but the relationships do not last. After a short time she is alone again. She looks with envy at her old schoolmates who found partners long ago and now have families. Will her dream man ever come along?

Those having difficulties in relationships should first look to their relationship with the parent of the same gender. Problems with current relationships often originate in damaged relationships with our same sex parent.

Traditional psychology suggests just the opposite: the relationship with the father is the influential factor for girls and for boys, the relationship with the mother. "He's still so dependant on his mother. No wonder he has problems with women," remark neighbors about the eternal bachelor. However, a man's most important step is not the inner separation from the mother, but rather, his bond with his father. A man gets the power to be a man only from his father.

Marie is good at flirting with men and wrapping them around her little finger. However, she lacks the mature, feminine strength to have a long-lasting relationship. So, despite her success at attracting men, all of her love relationships sooner or later end unhappily. What might Marie's relationship to her mother be like?

A strained relationship with the father or mother is usually a repeated pattern in one's family of origin system. An important and common systemic cause of disturbances in the relationship between parents and children is—unbelievable as this may sound—the *previous* love relationships (former partners, boyfriends, girlfriends) of the parents. These were not discussed in regards to the family of origin, because they are most influential in our *current* relationships.

> Marie never got along well with her mother. Added to that, she was always "daddy's little girl". Marie found out that her father was engaged to another woman before he married Marie's mother. After a long fight, he broke off that engagement and later married Marie's mother. In Marie's family, no one speaks about the woman her father was engaged to. The topic is taboo.

Even our parents' previous partners belong to our family of origin system, because they "made room" for the next partner, our father or mother. Without their departure, we would not be in this world. If a mother or father had been in a serious relationship before marriage, for example, if one of them had been in love with someone else, been engaged or had a previous marriage, then that previous partner also belongs to the system. In many families, past relationships are an unpleasant or awkward topic which is rather left alone. But if a previous partner is maligned or forgotten altogether, he or she will be represented by a child, in one or another future generation.

In her constellation, Marie stands close to her father. Both of them feel well connected and smile at each other. There is a palpable erotic tension between them. On the other hand, Marie feels distance between herself and her mother. When the previous fiancé is set up in the constellation, she and Marie smile pleasantly at each other.

In order to see whether or not Marie "represents" this previous fiancé, the therapist has them trade positions in the constellation. The fiancé then stands beside the father and it is immediately apparent that the father has strong feelings for the fiancé, because they cannot stop looking at each other. So Marie had, without anyone in her family knowing or recognizing it, "represented" her father's former fiancé. It is no wonder that she stands so close to her father in the constellation and doesn't feel like a daughter. The poor relationship with her mother also becomes understandable, because in Marie, the mother unconsciously senses her rival.

To release the tensions, the first important movement is to give the former fiancé the place in the family which belongs to her. The father is asked to bow slightly to her and say, "You are my first woman. You have a place in my heart as my first woman." Then he introduces his wife and children. "This is the wife whom I took after you and these are the children we had together. Please, be happy for us." The fiancé feels honored and acknowledged and is able to look at Marie's father with happiness.

Then the father says to Marie, "Now my former fiancé has received a place with us and you can take your place as a child. You are just my daughter and this (points to Marie's mother) is your mother." Marie bows long and deep to her mother and says to her, "I honor you as my mother. I am only the child." The mother looks at Marie with appreciation. Marie then feels drawn to her mother. She takes tentative steps towards her mother and they hold each other in their arms.

Former partners are often "represented" in family life by children. A child like Marie, who represents a past partner, holds a special place with her father and because of that, secretly feels superior to her mother. The mother senses this hidden arrogance from her child and withdraws from it. Marie can only leave this special role when the fiancé, who actually belongs here and whom Marie represents, receives a place in the system. That is why it is so important when the father honors his former fiancé by saying "You are my first love. You have a place in my heart as my first love."

In order to heal the relationship between Marie and her mother, it is important that Marie take on her proper role as the child by saying, "I honor you as my mother. I am only the child." Bowing helps to express honor and respect, and at the same time, it reflects a desire to atone for her previous, presumptuous behavior.

Sometimes the relationship between a child and a parent is so burdened that the child's representative must kneel on the floor and bow down until his head touches the ground (or even lie on his belly, arms outstretched, palms up), and ask to be received as the parents' child again. In this way, a deeply disturbed relationship can be healed.

The same dynamic is also found between mothers, sons and fathers. For instance, perhaps the mother had an intense relationship with a man at some point before she married her present husband. Again, it doesn't matter if this was teen love, an engagement or an actual first marriage. Her son may represent this first love. A constellation reveals this through the special place the son takes, in the position of the husband. This results on one hand, in an unusually deep relationship between the mother and son and on the other hand, a disturbed relationship between the father and son, due to the sense of rivalry between them. Only when the first love is set up in the constellation and given his place within the system, can the son be free from the burden of that role.

How can a child's relationship with his parents be strengthened and healed? There is a special type of constellation that gives strength to sons and daughters and allows masculine and feminine energies to flow. However, the two prerequisites are that other disturbing factors must first be removed and that the main tensions, or entanglements have already been resolved.

> The constellation starts with the mother standing behind her daughter. The grandmother stands behind the mother and behind the grandmother stands the great-grandmother. Similarly, the father stands behind the son, then the grandfather, then the great-grandfather. The most effective line goes back 7 generations. Each leans back on the person behind, feeling strong and supported at the same time.

The effect is even stronger when *all* of the forefathers of the same gender, those from both sides of the family, are placed behind the child. In other words, the father stands behind the son, then both of the son's grandfathers, then all four of the son's great-grandfathers, etc. Similarly, the mother would stand behind the daughter, then the two grandmothers, then the four great-grandmothers etc. The child standing at the front closes his or her eyes and accepts the feminine or masculine energy that flows to him or her through the generations.

Parenthood

The bond between a man and woman is not a purpose in and of itself. The purpose is to create a third. Unless thwarted, biological instincts drive us to the natural fulfillment of procreation.

> Mary is the single mother of a seven-year-old son, Michael. She lived with his father, Andrew, for two years and they separated after a fight. "Actually, he was never the right one," Mary would tell her friends. The first year after they were separated, Andrew helped take care of Michael, but then he stopped visiting. Mary had to continually demand payment of child support. Her only comment was, "That's just like a man. But my Michael," she continued, "will be completely different. I'm going to make sure he doesn't grow up to be like his father." In spite of this "intention", she has had continual problems with Michael since he entered school. He is hyperactive, unable to concentrate and physically aggressive, with the other children.

In my seminars, I encounter many single mothers. It seems as though more and more fathers choose to relinquish their responsibilities to the child after the breakup, for a variety of reasons. In Mary's constellation, one such dynamic comes into play.

> In the constellation, Michael is standing close to his mother. The father, Andrew, stands far away, facing the other direction. He feels as though he has been put off by Mary and is irritated. Michael feels as though he is standing too close to his mother and is also irritable. Mary feels no acknowledgement from Andrew and is very angry.

> [Reminder: Although the names of the people represented are used, it is actually representatives of those people taking part in the constellation.]

In constellations, this kind of anger usually only appears when there has been hardship or some type of emotional injury. Mary, observing the constellation from the sidelines, is asked by the therapist if there is a concrete reason for her anger that comes from her history with Andrew. Mary states that there is no particular reason. In the absence of any reason, such strong anger or rage is often found to have been taken over from another family member.

> In order to untangle this conflict and resolve it, first Mary stands facing Andrew and bows down slightly in acknowledgement. She slowly says to him, "I thank you for that which I received from you and what you received from me you may gladly keep. I take my part of the responsibility for our relationship not working out, and I leave you your part of the responsibility. I give you a place in my heart as my former husband and through our son, we remain connected."

Andrew then bows to Mary and says the same to her, as his former wife. Already, a large part of the tension has been resolved by these words and actions. As Andrew notices that he still feels some pain and anger, Mary can look at him and say openly to him, "I'm sorry." With that, Andrew's pain and anger is dissolved. Now both of them are able to stand beside each other in peace and look together at their son.

An important step, during and after a relationship, is for each partner to honor the other. Honoring the other partner after a separation is practically indispensable if a child was born from that union. Otherwise the child becomes the victim of the tension between the parents. What does a "good" separation look like? One must face the fact that every separation is painful. How can one honorably accomplish the separation? The statements used above in the constellation, show the way to a good resolution.

"I thank you for what I received from you and you may gladly keep what you received from me." With that, the focus is on the positive aspects from the common past. Especially in long relationships, the partners have experienced much together, both joy and pain. Apart from the negative, love has flowed in both directions. At the beginning, hopes, dreams and wishes were shared, even if they later turned to disappointment. Both the good and the challenging aspects are deserving of gratitude.

"I accept my part of the responsibility for the failure of our relationship and I leave your part of that responsibility to you." This simple declarative sentence relieves the most tension. It puts one simple reality up front. There are always two people responsible for the failure of a relationship. There is never an instance where one person is innocent. Most people forget this truth in the storm of feelings that arise during and after a break-up. Full of rage, we focus on the other and count our former partner's mistakes. He or she is completely to blame. An hour later our mood changes and we blame ourselves. Assuming and declaring our share of the blame allows our partner to take on his or her share as well. It's a great relief when the "blame game" finally ends.

"I give you a place in my heart as my former husband." Past partners belong to the system. They cannot willfully be shut out. If they are regarded with love and honor and "given a place in our hearts," it is good for both partners. Then it is not necessary that a former partner be represented later by a child, because he already has his place of honor in the system. From there, he can slowly, with time, move further away and be happy for the former partner and his or her new life. Distancing in this way is not possible if the former couple had children together, because children become a common thread between the mother and father that cannot be dissolved. This truth is expressed by Mary's last sentence, "And through our son we remain connected."

Things that are not cleared up between the parents burden the children. Often the child feels torn between the two parents, as if they must choose one or the other. It is especially damaging when the parents try to make the child an "ally" in their war against the other. In order to clarify that, the family constellation involving Mary, Andrew and Michael goes one step further.

> Mary stands beside Andrew and Michael stands facing them. Mary says to Michael, "What is between your father and me, we will work out between us."

Michael exhales, relieved. Mary continues, "You are only the child. You can have me for your mother and him for your father. You do not have to choose between us. You have us both." Michael is visibly happier after hearing this and looks from one parent to the other. Then he says to the parents, "I take you both as my parents. What is between you is not my problem. I am only the child."

A child faces an unsolvable dilemma when he has to choose one parent over the other. Children forced into such situations will often have problems making decisions as adults. Even small decisions in everyday life will give rise to the old predicament—how can I choose?

A child is always loyal to both parents, father and mother. On the surface, he may have decided to be loyal only to one, but on the inside, as well as with his behavior, he remains tied to the other parent as well. That is why, after a separation, it is important that the child be allowed access to both parents, with as little conflict as possible. The parents' relationship, with its problems and discord, belongs to them and has nothing to do with the child, nor should the child get involved.

As long as Mary does not honor Michael's father and wants Michael on her side, Michael will feel torn apart. No wonder Michael is aggressive at school! In the constellation, Mary removes a huge burden from Michael with the statements, "You are only the child. You can have me as your mother and him as your father. You do not have to choose between us. You have us both." Michael now knows that he does not have to choose between them, but rather, he has both parents. For him, this is the single most important thing.

Children connect parents to each other for good. The child is the fruit of the love the parents shared at the time of conception. That love is embodied in the child. A man who is not able to honor his present or past wife, girlfriend or lover, will not be able to honor the feminine side of his daughter. And the woman who cannot honor her present or past husband, boyfriend or lover, will not honor the masculine side of her son. That is why it is so important to honor one's former partner. By doing so, one honors the half of one's child that comes through the other parent.

Orders in Partnership and Parenthood: Who Takes Precedence?

A child is the responsibility of both the mother and father. If a man becomes a father and then lets the mother raise the child alone, he is dodging his responsibility and committing an injustice. The inner authority within him which maintains equilibrium will exact a price.

Through children, especially strong bonds are created between the parents, regardless of the other realities. The tie between the parents through the youngest (most recent) child is the strongest and has priority over any earlier bond between either of the parents and a previous relationship they may have had or still be in.

Let's say a couple lives in close relationship for years but there are no children born to that relationship. The man has an affair with another woman and she becomes pregnant. According to the new tie, this man should leave his current relationship to be with the new woman and child. If he decides to remain in the current relationship, that relationship as they have known it is dissolved, and a new relationship will emerge.

Because of this, every affair, including ones where there is no love, brings the risk of this new tie through a new child. Perhaps this helps explain why the jealousy over a "small" affair can be so strong. Every affair during childbearing years brings the risk of a pregnancy—the risk that a new tie will replace the current one. "Cheating" on a partner risks that relationship, every time. From this point of view, the partner's jealously, this mixture of fear, anger and other feelings, is not surprising.

In family constellations, the strength of the bond between parents and children can be seen. Motherhood and fatherhood as biological facts are enough to form this enduring bond with the child. Such a bond will exist even between a child and a father whom the mother encountered only briefly. This bond is of the same strength to either mother or father. Although on the surface, children may seem mostly attracted to the parent of the same sex, underneath there is a deeper level— an equally strong bond of loyalty to the other parent as well.

Under usual circumstances, it is good for a child to be raised by both parents. If that is not possible, then it is best that the child be raised by the parent who is able to honor the other parent, in that child. Children are equally well raised by fathers. If neither parent is able to care for the child, the next-best choice is the grandparents and after that, other relatives of the father or mother, for example an aunt or an uncle. Due to problems that arise from radically severing the bond between parents and children, adoption is beneficial only in extreme cases. However, foster parents are a good alternative, when they respect the existing bond with the true parents.

The partner's love for each other is the fertile ground for loving the children, and in the family, the partner comes before the child. The partner takes the "first place," and the child comes second. The child's wellbeing depends on the strength of the parents' partnership. Sometimes both partners put the child first, which does neither the child nor the parents any good. When a child takes precedence over the partner, it damages the relationship with the partner as well as with the child.

> In one family constellation, the father came home seriously ill after being held prisoner of war. At the same time, one of his children lay sick in a faraway hospital. The mother wanted to go to her child, but she remained with her husband, who was deathly ill. The child died without the mother being present. The woman decided she would never forgive herself, or her husband.
>
> A change for the better came when she said to her child, in the family constellation, "You were sick and your father was sick. I stayed with him, because he comes first." For the child, that was okay. She told that to her husband as well and suddenly, her feelings of guilt disappeared. The relationship between her and her husband improved also.

This is an extreme example. Normally, mothers and fathers sacrifice for the children, when that is necessary. This order changes if the parents separate and one or both find a new partner. The love from the parent to his own child will then take precedence over the love of the parent for the new partner. If this order is not attended to, the new relationship is destined for difficult, troubled times. Often, the new partner does not honor this priority of the love. They would prefer to take "first place" themselves. However, that is only possible if the two partners later have their *own* child together. It can be hard for a new partner, in a relationship with someone who has a child. Only when the order of precedence is respected are all of those involved able to relax. This example from one of my seminars demonstrates this phenomenon:

> The new girlfriend had a four-year-old son. It was clear to the man that his position in the relationship was second to that of the child and he truly did not want to disrupt that. From the beginning, the son was not jealous of him. Even when the man came to spend the night and the child was deprived of sleeping in the mother's bedroom, the boy complained a little but did nothing more. Thanks to the man's attitude, the son remained relaxed and friendly, even when he was displaced for a short time. Instead of conflict, there was mutual understanding.

There is one important thing to note, and this is complimentary to rather than contradictory to the previous paragraphs. A child should not come between the partners in their love-relationship. What is between man and woman is something special. A child does not in any way belong in that part of the relationship.

In addition, another order is important for success in this type of relationship. Hellinger says:

> For a couple's relationship to succeed, both of the partners must leave the family of origin. Not just in the physical sense, but also, each must let go of some values which applied in their family, and work out new values with their partner which will be suitable for both families. On this new level, the couple can have a relationship. Some people say things like, "My family is okay, but my partner's family is not." This works like poison in the relationship. When we marry, we marry our partner's family as well. This

means that we must honor and love our partner's family in the same way that we love the partner. Only then can love succeed.

Childlessness

If partners who are able to have children decide not to conceive and give birth, this weakens their bond to one another. To want a child and be unable to have one, however, is a difficult fate, which, if carried consciously, joins a couple together and brings them closer. On the other hand, one partner who does not want a child or is infertile, has no right to stop the other from leaving so that he or she may have a child. In that case, he or she must let the other go. Hellinger states:

> Generally, when we choose one thing, we are choosing to let go of something else. That which we choose is that which will be realized . . . if we do not honor that which has *not* been realized, then this takes something away from that which has been chosen. It becomes less. If we honor that which has not been realized, even though we chose not to do it, then we add something to that which we *have* chosen. Women who consciously decide not to have children, who are aware of their loss and agree to the decision, retain their femininity. It has a different quality. Something is gained, in that case, when one decides *consciously* not to have children. That which I did not choose has a positive influence when I honor it.

When a person chooses one alternative in life (parenthood, for example), the other alternative should also be honored. The woman who remains childless should honor the mother within. Growth comes when a person is willing to accept the pain and the loss associated with what has been given up (e.g., motherhood).

The Bond to Previous Partners

Love fails, relationships end, partners leave each other, new partners are found, new relationships begin. How can we deal constructively with past partners? Let's expand on the information from the last section.

> Renée separated from her partner John and is now living with her new boyfriend, Roland. Roland is jealous of John and has only negative things to say about him. Just for the sake of smoothing things over and having peace, Renée also talks negatively about John.
>
> The relationship between Renée and Roland was a very happy one at first, but both are becoming more and more dissatisfied. Neither of them knows why things are going sour.

When a couple begins, they must honor each others former partners. John was Renee's last partner. When someone complains about or curses their last partner, this damages the new relationship. When Renée talks poorly about her first partner, she burdens her relationship with Roland, even though Roland encourages such talk about. John. When a former partner is denigrated, the new partner knows, on some level, that he may suffer the same fate at some time in the future. Renée carries this tension into her new relationship with Roland.

Unconsciously, secretly, the new partner always feels a certain solidarity with those who came before him—in this case with John—because, being a man, he is not that different from John himself. Likewise, when Roland talks poorly of *his* former partners, Renée remembers what he really thinks of women, after the first few exciting weeks are over. This solidarity with the same sex sometimes goes so far that a person does not allow himself to completely love or trust the new partner because of their awareness of previous injustices to others like him or her.

It is also important for each person to honor their new partner's former partners. If the former partners are somehow "cheapened" and looked down upon, the unspoken judgment is that the person chose poorly. The new partner is also saying in effect that he is better than the former and behaves as if this were true.

> During the constellation, John is standing at Renée's side, turned away. Roland is standing on the other side of Renée, very close. Both feel the discomfort of their proximity to one another. In order to relieve the tension, Renée moves away from Roland and then looks toward John. She bows lightly to him and says, "I honor you as my former partner." John feels happy when she says this and Renée, too, feels more relaxed. She then gestures to Roland, as if she is introducing him to John and says, "This is my new partner, please be happy for us." Although John is able to look happily at Renée, he is not yet able to look towards Roland in a friendly manner.
>
> Roland still feels jealous. In the next step, Roland stands in front of John, bows slightly and says, "You came before me. I came after you. I honor you and your place." Roland then feels less jealous and John is able to look at him in a friendly way.

When Renée honestly honors John as her former partner, she makes peace with him and with herself. Now the old partner can look kindly at the new relationship and wish them well.

The bows and declarations are important for Roland as well. The first partner takes the first place and the others follow in chronological order. Each person and their place must be honored. This is not about being "better" or "worse"—nor is it judgmental. Anyone wanting to "force his way to the front" or come across as superior to previous partners, will create tension and damage the new relationship. As in previous examples, neither Roland nor John was present in the constellation, but resolution may affect them both nonetheless.

When someone knows that one or more partners came before, he may prefer to have been the first, but he is not. He may be the second or third or fourth. That is simply how life is. It is important to see this and accept it. When a person does not honor the place of his predecessor(s), he undermines the new relationship. If both partners act as if the first partner(s) did not exist, they are deceiving themselves and this disturbs the current relationship.

All previous partners belong to the larger system. Existing tensions between current and former partners in a family can be revealed and resolved in a constellation. When they have been resolved and the previous partners all have "a good place," they often become a support, a source of energy. "A good place" means that they are honored and respected as previous partners and as predecessors, each in their rightful position.

Among past partners, which ones are relevant in the family system? Everyone with whom ties were created belongs to the system. Spouses, fiancés and other important relationships are counted among relevant past partners. A partner with whom a person created a child definitely belongs to the system—even if the child was the product of a brief relationship. When two people have sex, with or without love, a bond is created, whether they want it or not.

Hellinger describes the meaning of sexuality as follows:

> Some people feel that sexuality is a bad thing. However, it is a powerful drive and it is irresistible. Sexuality propagates life against all obstacles. In this way, sexuality is greater than love. And of course, it is especially great when it is done with love.

In the course of family constellation work, I have also seen deep bonds between people who have not had sex. This usually happens during youth. A teen-aged boyfriend and girlfriend may not have had sex, but a deep tie was created between them nonetheless—possibly strengthened by the unrequited sexual tension. The heart may be "possessed" by that first love and the next person stands little chance. It makes sense to set up and resolve this type of former relationship.

Bert Hellinger, in discussion, was skeptical about this point of view. According to his experience, a permanent bond to a partner occurs only if there has been sex. He has seen it happen that the memory of a young love is used as an excuse to secretly rid oneself of a current partner. According to Hellinger, this is actually a refusal of the partner, and can be exposed in a family constellation.

Family constellations often give us a fascinating picture of "first love." It may have taken place ten, twenty or thirty years before, and yet the representatives glow as they look at each other and show how strong their attraction to each other remains. Astonishing bonds become visible and often the person setting up the constellation was not conscious of the strength of this connection to their past.

The bond is often strongest in the first relationship. With each break-up and with each new relationship, the bond weakens. Bit by bit, the strength of subsequent bonds lessen. However, in this sense the bond with a partner and the love for a partner differ from one another. Hellinger states:

> "It (the second love relationship) does not have the depth of the first one. It cannot and it doesn't need to. This does not mean that each subsequent relationship will be less happy or less loving. The love in the second relationship can and may be greater and deeper than that of the first. It is just that a bond or a connection like that in the first relationship is denied them.

Family constellations repeatedly demonstrate that over-dependence on a partner does not reflect a mature connection. Such dependence is similar to the relationship between a child and a parent, rather than between adults. If someone declares his partner to be the only one possible ("If you leave me, I won't survive"), this burdens the relationship. There is not just one true partner. To quote Hellinger, "It is seldom that one finds 'Mr. Right' or 'Miss Right.' Usually, it is enough to find 'a good man' or 'a good woman.' However, partners are sometimes strongly interwoven with one another and to a degree, everyone holds on to his partner, like a child with his parents, feeling helpless and vulnerable without the other.

> During the family constellation, husband and wife stand across from each other. Behind them, the man's mother and the woman's father are set up. The

man turns around and for a while looks alternately at his mother and at his wife, so that he learns to differentiate the two. Then he says to his mother, "You are my mother." He then turns to his wife and says, "And you are my wife." He then says to the wife, "Your father is standing behind you. I am only your husband." After that, the wife makes the corresponding statements to her husband.

In a partnership, it is sometimes necessary to make these differences clear. Spoken aloud, these declarations provide insight and unburden both partners.

It also impedes a mature relationship when one feels overly responsible for his or her partner and is consequently willing to carry their partner's entire ancestral family burden. With regard to family "baggage", it is best if the man bows to the woman and says, "I honor you and that which you carry and I leave it to you. I am only your husband (boyfriend/lover/partner)." The woman then bows in return and makes the corresponding statements to her partner. Rather than distance, these statements result in the freedom to get closer.

A relationship leads to a bond, and every bond seeks a lasting connection, namely, marriage. If one partner wants marriage and the other does not, this is experienced as an "illness" which corrodes the relationship and can cause it to fail. Hellinger asks those who have had a relationship lasting several years, "Why aren't you married? Are you waiting for someone better to come along?"

Entanglements and feelings which have been taken over are systemic problems which also influence our choice of partners. The power of this influence is enormous. Most people find a partner who "fits in" with the familial influences. In the best case, each partner gives protection and stability to the other and in the worst case, they cannot stand being with each other and the relationship is destroyed.

Hellinger warns against blaming the other during a separation:

> When people break up, no one person is to blame. Usually, a relationship ends because each person is entangled in some way with the family, or because a person is on another "path" or being led or drawn to another. However, if one of the parties is blamed, both have the view and illusion that there is something that could have been done about it, or that each just needed to behave in a different way and the relationship would have been saved. Then the depth and breadth of the situation is not recognized and instead, each looks for blame in the other. The solution is for both to accept the deep pain and sadness that the relationship is over, each in their own way, each accepting their own responsibility for the break-up.

Almost every break-up is very painful. Aside from looking for blame, the ego has another mechanism which hinders one from feeling the full pain of the break-up—anger. Anger is a feeling which is easier to tolerate than pain. As long as a person is angry, they don't feel the pain and the loss. Only when one lets go of the anger, and stops blaming the other, can he face the pain, sadness and loss.

Abortion

In Germany, as well as in many other countries, abortion is a heavily fought over topic on the battlefield of ideology. The positions taken on this subject range from "my body belongs to me" to "abortion is murder." With family constellations, we leave the world of ideologies. When one sees an aborted child represented in a constellation, it sheds new light on the abortion debate from a different perspective. The effect of an abortion can be uncovered by observing the representatives in the family constellation. Through this lens, one can find the necessary steps toward a solution.

Aborted children belong to the present family system, i.e., a person's *own* aborted child is set up. Aborted children, however, do not belong to the family of origin system, i.e. if my father and mother had an aborted child, that child is not set up among my siblings. It is the parent's decision—their issue— and generally has nothing to do with the other children.

> Raymond and Irene already have three children and do not want any more, although Irene recently became pregnant. Both of them believe that the best solution is to abort the child and they do so. At first, after the abortion, Irene was not doing well, but then she returned to normal. "I did what was best for all of us," she said to herself and then returned to everyday life. However, her relationship with Raymond suddenly became more trying. They did not get along as well as they used to and they closed themselves off from one another.

Family constellations, when done in western cultures, show that abortions are often perceived as a trespass against someone or as an injustice. One's inner authority prevents any type of influence or argument against this. Nor does it allow for justification. It works independently of any of these arguments. However, awareness of the injustice of this act is often suppressed in the soul.

Nonetheless, the inner authority strives for "payback" or "atonement." Sometimes, the abortion is "paid for" with the breakup of the relationship or the interruption of sex in the relationship. In addition, when only one partner wants the abortion, they are often making a negative statement about the partner (i.e., "I don't want your child.")

> During the constellation, the aborted child is set up behind Irene and Raymond. The child feels very cold and cut off from the parents.
>
> The first step towards healing comes when the therapist brings the child to the foreground, so that it can be seen. Raymond becomes very sad when he looks the child in the eye and at first Irene looks away. However, the child now feels somewhat better. Then the child sits on the floor and leans back against both parents.
>
> Irene still feels cut off from the situation and from the child. There seems to be something between Irene and the child which needs clearing up. After questioning Raymond, it becomes clear that Irene secretly blamed Raymond, because he did not try to stop the abortion. She says to him, "I blame you for not stopping the abortion."
>
> It seems as though Irene refuses to acknowledge and carry her part of the responsibility. That is why Raymond then says to her, "I will carry my responsibility for the abortion and I leave you yours." She says the same thing to him. After that, they are able to stand beside each other in a more relaxed manner.
>
> Irene then looks down at the child and says, "You are the child that we aborted. You gave me the most that a person could give—your life. I accept that you made room and I carry my guilt and responsibility." With these sentences, Irene's pain becomes even greater. Then she says, "I give you a place in my heart." Both parents then look at the child and feel

their sadness. Raymond takes Irene's hand and says
to her, "We will carry it together." With this, the child
feels accepted, safe and secure, knowing it is seen
and has a place with the parents.

In order to have inner peace after an abortion, the
aborted child must receive his place in the system of the
mother and father. At first, the most important thing is to be
able to see the child as an individual. When someone looks
the child in the eyes, the reasonable reaction is pain due to
the loss, guilt, ambivalence and other emotions. This pain
must be faced, because it heals. Then the person's own
responsibility and guilt is accepted and with that, a person
can gradually move on.

If only one partner wanted the abortion and forced it on
the other, the other partner secretly holds himself or herself
as guilt-free and the other as guilty, and withholds forgiveness. In this case, it is good when each person carries his or
her share of the responsibility. One expression which aids
forgiveness is, "We carry this responsibility together."

In my seminars, I frequently experience people who
want to avoid this. For example, one says, "Since then, I have
come to terms with the abortion. It is no longer a problem."
Or the esoteric variant, which also avoids reality, "Two years
after the abortion, I became pregnant again. I felt without
question that the child had the same soul as the aborted
child." This attitude is an attempt to avoid looking at the
aborted child, taking the responsibility for one's actions and
feeling the pain. Nevertheless, if the aborted child can be
seen, important steps toward healing may be taken.

Here is what Hellinger once had to say to the parents
after such a constellation:

"It needs some time, before the pain comes. Then let the pain have a place in the presence of the child. One can also give the child a place in one's life for a time. For example, in your mind's eye, you could show this child his siblings and for a time, perhaps a year, show him the beauty in the world. But then it must end. The guilt must pass after a certain time and after that, it doesn't need to be talked about any more. The child will have his peace, and you can look to the future."

Another example:

During a break in a seminar, the topic was the participant's relationship which had broken up. "For the most part," he said, "we always had arguments about the new dog that we got." As a joke, the participant said that perhaps they could set up the dog in the family constellation. It was clear where the dog would stand—at the feet of the owners.

Later, during the same constellation, the topic of abortion came up. The couple had had an abortion one year before the breakup. The aborted child, who was represented, then sat at the feet of the couple—just like the dog. They had gotten the dog shortly after the abortion. That dog exposed the conflict between the couple.

Sometimes an abortion is the reason that a couple is unable to find peace in a family constellation. Only when the abortion comes to light and the partners own it, can acceptance and peace be found.

Control Contradicts the
Essence of Relationships

I will end this chapter with an excerpt from an interview I conducted in 1995 with Bert Hellinger, in which he talks about relationships:

> *Q:* I want to start with a basic question on the topic of relationships. One can see in the family constellations that there are more and more broken relationships and families. We are seeing more and more ex-spouses or ex-boy or girlfriends. Life for couples is becoming more chaotic. Where do you see the causes? Where do you see the hope?

> *Hellinger:* To me, the question begs to be asked, whether we know why relationships are falling apart more often or not. I don't judge the phenomena that we see. If such a development occurs, then I assume that there is some order in it, because I have seen that it is impossible for anyone to go against order. If a person thinks that he must somehow restore something to what it once was, on some sort of principle, he often goes against the grain more than someone who simply agrees with a development as it is.

> *Q:* Your work seems to go in a direction where the element of bonds is emphasized, because it works with the existing bonds.

> *Hellinger:* I show that these bonds exist. However, the goal of the work is not to strengthen the bonds. That would be presumptuous of me. I only show the individuals the dynamic. Whether or not it helps them on their path through life, I don't know. But it doesn't matter, because all I do is look for the

order behind something and I leave the rest to the individual. However, I think that the failure of relationships must have some meaning in the collective development of humanity, just as the fact that man has alienated himself from nature must have some kind of meaning—a meaning which I don't know and don't even want to know. But I flow with the development of humanity as it is and that is why I do not try to recreate a way of life which is no longer lived today.

Q: You say that you flow with the development of humanity. Can you see a direction in which that development is going?

Hellinger: No. He who goes with the flow does not know where the river leads. He just flows with it.

Q: To you, how are love, sex and relationships related? If someone enters a relationship, what can they do to help it succeed? Do you have any advice on this?

Hellinger: These concepts are based on the idea that the relationship can be "steered" in a certain direction. For example, a person thinks that if he pays attention to certain things, then a certain result will follow. That is a type of control. That kind of control contradicts what a relationship is.

FOUR

Family Dynamics
in the United States

For Americans, even the title of this book may cause scepticism. "The Healing Power of the Past?" Isn't the past behind us while our eyes turn to the adventures of the future? Although this book was originally written only for German readers, for the English edition I decided to add material for American readers. In the many workshops that I have facilitated in the United States, I have learned about issues and dynamics unique to the US.

America is known as a "melting pot". Many different cultures, many different human fates meet there. Many contrasting dynamics result. This Introduction does not deal with all of them; it just gives some insights and some new thoughts.

Homelessness

One main issue for Americans is the capacity to move again and again without establishing a real *home* city or state.

While this seems natural for Americans, it is astonishing to foreigners. In family constellations, we discover the roots of what can be seen as flexibility or restlessness, depending on your point of view. An example:

> The client comes with great sadness for her eldest daughter because she is a heroin addict. We set up the mother (the client), her husband and the daughter.
>
> The parents stand before their child. The mother feels pulled towards her, while the child feels pulled from behind. I ask if there have been special facts (traumatic events) in the family of the mother. Nothing. I then add the maternal grandmother and she expresses that she feels very weak.
>
> The weakening forces seem to come from further back so I ask about the family roots. The maternal great-grandmother emigrated with her husband from Italy to the United States. I place a representative for the home country—Italy—behind them. This brings great relief to everyone in the constellation and the mother gets the impression that she can see her child for the first time. Everyone turns to Italy and acknowledges her as the country from where the family came.
>
> However, the daughter begins to feel worse and worse. She feels cramps in her belly. A strange image of seasickness arises. I ask the great-grandmother and she feels lonely, abandoned and also seasick like her great-grandchild. She says: "I feel helpless. In my life I could never do what I wanted." Suddenly she gets very thirsty, as if she nearly died of thirst during her overseas journey. I propose to her the sentences, "It was too much. A part of me stayed back in Italy". She agrees and spontaneously adds, "I think I also took drugs." (Later on we suspected she took laudanum, a drug commonly used in that time to calm the nerves).

The great-granddaughter steps to the side of the grandmother and feels sick, like her. The great-grandmother looks lovingly at the child. Then the child bows before her great-grandmother, acknowledging her pain, then steps back and feels very relieved.

Now I bring the great-grandfather to his wife's side. At first it is not easy, but after some work, they look friendlier towards each other and to the later generations. Slowly, peace comes to the family and we finish the constellation.

What can we understand about the roots of Americans from this and many similar constellations? For many immigrants who came to America, it was a profound and painful event to leave their country. Not many came from lust for adventure. Most came to survive. In the struggle to survive in their new country, they had to suppress the longing for their homeland. And they found they felt stronger when looking forward rather than back. But deep inside, the pain of being uprooted remained.

Children are loyal to their parents. If they plant roots in their new American homeland, they feel as though they have betrayed and abandoned their parents. This loyalty demands that the children, grandchildren and great-grandchildren move, like their ancestors before them, perpetuating the sense of having no roots.

The paradox for the Americans is that this loyalty to the forefathers obliges them to cut off their roots. "I am faithful as long as I do not look back or feel the strong bonds to my homeland".

There is a lot of tension underneath this behavior, as passionate feelings are repressed and the conflict of the forefathers is adopted. How can peace be found? Feelings cannot be suppressed totally and forever. They are passed on in a family system. Constellations reveal a unique solution. The children look back to where these emotions began.

The descendants must allow themselves to come in contact with the trauma experienced by the first emigrating generation. They face their family members and see their pain. At the same time, they may feel a connection with and love for their ancestors, who had to leave their homeland. Honoring what these ancestors did is the natural next step and bowing before them is an adequate expression of this. Then, in the constellation, someone may ask the first immigrants for their blessing, while they relax and become more grounded. What happens? The ancestors give their blessing in a friendly and very benevolent manner.

This does not mean that now you have to lose your flexibility, stay put and grow roots! The new conscious connection with your ancestors helps you to be more grounded in yourself. From that place, you have more options—you can move or you can stay. Either way, you are out of the grip of an unconscious drive.

The Rootless Become Ruthless

When the immigrants came to the United States, they did not find an uninhabited country. The genocide of the Native Americans is an important aspect of American history. All actions carry consequences. If perpetrators refuse to take responsibility for the consequences of their actions, their children carry this burden. So what exactly are the consequences? My comments are in parentheses in the following example.

The client is a woman whose father comes from Europe and whose mother comes from a Native American tribe. She has had eight car accidents in the last few years. She states that her mother's tribe fought her father's ancestors, who had come from Europe and had fought the Native Americans.

We set up a representative for the client (the daughter), one for the Europeans (hereafter called "he") and one for the Native Americans (hereafter called "she").

The representative of the Native Americans stands in front. She feels pulled forward and unsure of what is behind her, where the representative of the Europeans stands. He wants to slowly withdraw. Between them is the daughter who feels torn between two very powerful forces. Finally, the daughter stands next to the Europeans and feels better there. The Native Americans become very agitated, look back and tell the daughter, "I want you by my side." The daughter goes there. (A child can never find peace while in the middle of the parents' conflict. When the conflict is so enormous, as it is between the European conquerors and the Native Americans, the child is overwhelmed by her desire to fix it – "I'll do it for you".)

The Europeans do not want to see it. The representative closes his eyes, looks down and hangs his head. Then he says "I feel shame," goes down to his knees and starts to cry. By looking in the eyes of the Native Americans, the Europeans realize what they have done.

The Native Americans say to the child, "Only half of you comes from me, the other half comes from the Europeans. You are also part of that." The child feels terrible and does not know where to go. One part of her wants to go down to the ground, the other side fights against it. She feels only pain. The Native

Americans, who feel superior towards the Europeans, who is on his knees, say to him, "I like you at my feet."

The child comes closer to the Europeans, who is lying on the ground now, cries and tells him, "You killed so many of us!" (This shows the child's identification with her Native American ancestors.) Now the Native Americans, feeling very weak in the knees, tell the child that this burden is not hers. "We take our pain back and carry it. Our people experienced death and suffering. You are not entitled to carry it for us, you are only the child." This makes it clearer for the child and comes as a great relief. She bows before them, feeling better and more connected to her Native American ancestors.

The Europeans wake up when this happens and the representative wants to be included in it. But the child feels connected only to the Native Americans and wants nothing to do with the Europeans. She says to him, "Whatever is wrong with me comes from you."

The Europeans cannot deal with this. He is not really available to the child and feels the need to go back to his roots. I propose that he look back where he came from. He turns and looks back. (From my experience, I know that this allows one to look back into the past and to feel the influence of the past on the present.) He says, "I feel a pain in my heart," and walks thirty feet in the direction of the past. There his head drops. He appears broken when facing whatever happened back in Europe. (We can imagine the difficult lives people left behind for their dream of America.)

I suggested he say, "I will get even." (Former victims or their descendants turn easily into perpetrators. They give what their ancestors had to take.) Immediately he changes and shouts, "I grow stronger and stronger and stronger and then I will get even." An enormous cry comes from his throat, "I am not a victim and I will never be a victim again."

The Europeans go still further in the direction of the past. He feels such heartache as he connects to his ancestors. He tells them, "I remain loyal to you no matter what."

The child is watching the scene and feels compassion for him. The Native Americans are not content. She wants him to face her directly. She waits for him.

The Europeans persist in not looking. Instead he wants to leave the room, feeling both stubbornness and despair. He says, "I don't know what to do."

The child becomes very impatient, tired and angry, "I want you to stand up straight! It is better to fight then to be weak. Look at me!" (Again the child shows loyalty to the Native Americans.)

But the Europeans go out the door. I follow him and outside he tells me, "Here I feel free. I don't want anyone to tell me what to do. I would rather leave!" (Making demands doesn't open someone's heart.)

So, I suggested the child say to him, "I am part of you and I honor you and your pain and your escape." Suddenly, he comes back and looks at her. The child bows to him in honor. After that the child feels great relief. (Relief comes not with demands, but with honoring.)

Now the Europeans stand before the Native Americans. He starts to cry loudly, tears coming down his face. He reaches out to the Native Americans. She stands with open hands, comes slowly, slowly closer and takes the hands of the crying Europeans. He bows before her then they both stand side by side and turn towards the child.

The child is truly shocked to see them together. Both ancestors tell the child, "In you we are together. You do not need to choose between us." And the Europeans add, "Something new can come out of our togetherness." Finally the client takes the place of her representative, comes forward to both the Native Americans

> and the Europeans, closes her eyes, leans back on
> them ands feels how they come together in her.

This constellation unfolded over forty minutes. Some important American issues were touched. You can see how the past, when denied, has an ongoing effect on relationships in the present. It is so hard for the "perpetrator" to look into the eyes of the "victim" and see an equal human being. And most essential, the present generation feels the need to continue the fight of the forefathers. It's easier to be blind, stubborn and hard-hearted then to look back to them and see what they suffered and what they did. The children are not partners or allies in the fight or suffering—they are only descendants. Bowing makes them small as they look back to the past.

The root of ruthlessness is suppressed pain. The cruellest person can be a former victim in his blind fight against being victimized again. While the original victim may be too destroyed to fight, the descendants adopt the pain and aggression. And they still feel like victims and see the others as perpetrators. This makes them in a certain way "blind" and they feel entitled to fight without mercy. You can see this dynamic in Israel.

There are additional examples in American history which show how the past influences the present and how the memory of victimization stays in families. I facilitated only a few constellations with African Americans. While the constellation work has already reached some groups of Native Americans, it seems it will take some time until constellations reach into the culture of African Americans. It seems evident from the little work that I have done in this area, that enslaving a population surpasses murder in its deleterious effects on the dignity of the victim.

An African American client was feeling a lot of anger and stress and wanted to feel more at peace. When I ask for some facts, she says that the great-grandfather killed the great-grandmother. They were the first generation which gained their freedom from slavery. I placed the client and her great-grandparents. The couple looked at each other with enormous hatred. I wondered "Where does such hatred come from? Certainly it has to do with their history." So I propose that the man say to his wife, "I could not protect you." He says that and feels enormous shame. The woman replies to him, "You could not protect me. I am filled with disgust and contempt." In slavery, a person's dignity is destroyed. Instead of directing the hatred toward the slave owners, the hatred goes inside, towards oneself and one's own people.

So, I bring in the facts by proposing they say to each other, "You were a slave and I was a slave." The air fills with heaviness and darkness. Both have tears in their eyes. I give them the sentence, "It was unbearable, it was too much." And the man says, "Out of this despair, I killed you." The woman now looks to him with loving eyes and takes his hand. They stand side by side. The client comes in and bows before their pain and their fate. She asks them for their blessing. "Please look friendly upon me when I find peace." Both grandparents look friendly and wish the best for their great-granddaughter.

The facts surrounding slavery are connected with pain, hatred and shame, and this destroys or impedes the natural bond of affection between a man and a woman. So a man withdraws from his wife and children, suppresses his natural desire to take care of his family and is rejected by the woman because of her own wounds. The children carry these feelings on.

When somebody looks back, feels the enormous heaviness and honors what happened, then a solution begins. Sometimes in a constellation, a very heavy stone is used as a symbol for the burden carried unconsciously by later generations for those who came before. The client takes this heavy stone/burden carried throughout their life, looks with love and compassion into the eyes of the ancestors, slowly approaches them, bows and places the stone with respect at their feet.

Guilt and Becoming Adult

The word guilt has come to be used in family constellations in a unique way. Constellations have shown me more facets of the word and how inevitable it is as a part of human existence. How can "guilt" best be defined? You may feel guilt when you harm somebody physically or emotionally. Despite the reasons and justifications supplied by the head, there is an inner authority which reacts independently of such reason.

At the same time, to feel innocent is one of our strongest desires. Bert Hellinger says "The child needs for the parents to say 'You are good.' A person like this looks only to the parents and not to reality. He can not distinguish what is good or evil in the sense of supporting life or impeding life. He cannot break away from the reality supported by his family. If he does, he feels guilty." Therefore, we avoid responsibility in the hopes of avoiding guilt.

Guilt arises often in the natural flow of life because human beings are not perfect. It is not in our power to avoid ever harming someone. Parents feel stressed and hurt their children out of their impatience. Couples fight and hurt each other out of their own pain and confusion. Even a therapist could say, "There is a client that I could not help, perhaps because of my own limitations, lack of experience or knowledge or because of the burdens I carry from my own family." The client leaves—and is hurt. Is guilt to be an expected feeling for the therapist? The arguments I hear in such situations sometimes sound shallow. "This is his responsibility." "In the long run, it is for the best." "There are no accidents."

And often, life shows us something more. It does not take bad intentions to feel guilty.

> The client feels homeless and looks for a link to his family. Asked about the facts in the family history he says that his father fought as a soldier in World War II. He added that his father's parents were of German origin and immigrated some years before to the United States. Listening to him, I felt the enormous internal conflict that his father must have felt, to come from Germany and then fight against his former countrymen. In the constellation, this conflict was felt by the representatives also. Is it ever possible to resolve such a conflict? What does one do? I let the father face the relatives he had left behind in Germany and proposed that he tell them, "I had to choose between betraying the United States, my new homeland, by not fighting against the Germans or fighting against you, my relatives. I decided to fight and accept the guilt." These sentences strengthened and relieved him.

Again and again life brings quandaries from which there is no escape without guilt. Every option brings guilt. We experience it in smaller things and in more substantial situations.

After many years in a neglected marriage, the man (or the woman) falls passionately in love with somebody else and wants to start a new relationship. Whether he goes or stays—in both situations he hurts someone—either his current partner or his new beloved. Guilt is inevitable.

Or knowing that Saddam Hussein kills innocent people—I do nothing and am in some way responsible for the victims or I bomb his country and kill innocent people. Guilt is inevitable. In this sense, also, the Civil War in the United States still casts a black shadow from the background. I have not yet had a constellation dealing with it, but I know from my colleagues, how influential this war can be in a family's history.

Still, to accept this responsibility is difficult and painful. So we justify our actions by saying, "It is not my fault, it is yours. Or, "This was my only option. It was the right thing to do!" In that way, we try to ease our burden and avoid seeing our actions and their consequences. We avoid looking into the eyes of the other person to keep our feeling of innocence.

If my inner authority judges my behavior as wrong, it will make sure that a balance happens. In a constellation, the representative feels this guilt and feels the pressure towards actions which balance. For example, someone who kills another human being may feel innocent in doing so, but inside he feels guilty and sees himself as murderer. If he does not accept his guilt and the consequences of his actions, his descendants take over the guilt and ensure that a balance is found.

By writing this, a strange idea comes to me. Perhaps the obesity prevalent in America reflects a certain balance with the millions who starve on the other side of the planet. Dispossession, murder and slavery form the basis of American history. Today so many young people mutilate themselves, shedding their blood in order to feel something, while women of all ages go under the knife as slaves to the cultural ideas of beauty. Doesn't it seem to reflect a certain balance? There may be other explanations, but looking from several perspectives is worthwhile.

How do you face your own guilt? Some years ago, Hellinger engaged in a prison project, going to a number of London jails, setting up constellations with the prisoners. I took part in one constellation.

> In this constellation the client was a murderer who had killed another man in a fight. The prisoner took me as representative for the victim and Gunthard Weber (a renowned German doctor, therapist and facilitator) for himself. We stood facing each other. I did not want to look at the perpetrator and felt an enormous rage. But I knew a harsh truth: I could have killed him also. It was more an accident that he killed me first.
>
> Then the perpetrator fell loudly crying to the ground. (After the constellation Gunthard said he never in his life had experienced such pain.) When I heard the sobbing, I became softer and felt compassion towards him. Finally I went to him and touched his shoulders. We looked at each other for a long time. The tears of my companion flowed freely. After a time, I had the feeling," now it is enough", and I slowly withdrew.

The essential element of this constellation for me was this: somebody did something bad to someone else, something which cannot be undone. The only solution for the perpetrator is to acknowledge the other, to look him in the eyes as another human being. Then an enormous pain rises in the perpetrator and he accepts it. He is changed by this, and a new peace comes to a difficult event.

One way to reach your guilt is to realize your need to feel innocent. On the other hand, going to the other extreme and seeing yourself only as guilty, is just another way of escaping. With self-condemnation, you remain focused on yourself and avoid looking into the eyes of the person you have hurt.

Becoming an adult or "growing up" in this regard, means to see your own guilt and take responsibility for your actions. Then you become more understanding and more compassionate towards others, something which was expressed in the bible: "Whosoever is without guilt shall throw the first stone."

The American Spirit

The American spirit carries the thrill of adventure, the pursuit of happiness. Nothing seems impossible. This gives great strength to the American people. There is a seemingly limitless optimism. A welcoming country for immigrants. The prospect of a vast horizon, a new world, holding limitless possibilities for all.

Is it possible to compare a nation with a human being? If we dare to do so, which state of human history would you give to the US? How do we compare the perspective of "old" Europe with the experiences coming from family constellations? Even if the ideas do not fit exactly, they may give some new directions in which to think.

The time where life seems to be an adventure is in the time of youth. Youth characteristically feels enormous power and invincibility with which to conquer life. These feelings are brought on by the hormonal changes of adolescence, changes which promote self-assurance and a sense of immortality. The certainty of doing better than the parents is undeniable, combined with an arrogance (as perceived by the adults) and disdain for the older generation. Because children and teens are created with keen observational skills, they can sniff out the lies adults tell and see the mounting frustration and resignation that comes with growing up. They are young and fresh and determined to fulfil their dreams. They do not want to be like their parents. They feel unique and want to be different.

This phase is very important and necessary for a young person. Only by going through it, can an adolescent move from dependence to autonomy. Staying in this state of rebellion and rejection, however, inhibits maturation. A part of him stays childlike. This part feels superior to the parents and sees himself as different from them. Under this presumption, he denies certain aspects of his own being, which he does not want to see. This becomes a barrier to his own growth.

What could that mean for a nation? In the work with constellations, Hellinger talks of "acknowledging what is". This starts with acknowledging one's dreams and visions. The next step is to look at what is here, now—the reality. For that, you must look in two directions, outside and inside. The most important is what's inside. The outer world repeatedly confronts you with what you don't want to see inside, which in turn clouds your vision of the outer world.

The old wisdom of the Greek oracle of Delphi still holds value as the most important law of life, "Know thyself." Self knowledge allows for an unbiased look at everything else. What hinders this detached, unprejudiced look is something Americans seem to value a lot—ego. The bigger the ego, the greater the barrier to self knowledge. The ego judges what is good and what is evil. Then one tries to increase the good and eliminate the evil. This is problematic. You can't seek to know and assimilate all the parts of yourself while denying those parts deemed unacceptable. This is a contradiction which inhibits self knowledge.

There seems to be a strong split between good and evil. To understand how somebody can act in an "evil" way is avoided for fear that understanding would encourage further evil. This judgement of good and evil inhibits understanding. One accepts the good without question and rejects the evil for fear of its influence.

I like very much the new direction of "Positive Psychology" developed by Seligman, Csikszentmihalyi and others. These men explore human growth and the way to a fulfilled life. But reading Seligman's book, *Authentic Happiness: Using the New Positive Psychology to Realize Your Potential for Lasting Fulfillment*, I am astonished at how much is written about virtues. And to achieve the virtues you have to develop character. This means you must challenge your weakness, laziness and dark side. In my experience this fight is an ongoing source of inner tensions. Especially so for Americans, with so much history as yet unacknowledged.

What can we find when we look at 9/11? 9/11 brought an enormous restlessness onto the scene for German constellation facilitators. There was an urge to do something by means of constellations to help, to change or to heal. Tragedies, in which many people die, show us in one moment, that life is not as safe as we would like to believe. Death can happen at any moment. When so many people are murdered at once, the shock is immense. Such criminal actions remind us of the "evil" in human beings.

But this "evil", the aggression, the blind, murderous rage and the vengefulness belong to each of us. In constellations, I encounter murderous energy again and again as part of each family. And we are connected with these members of our family as well. We have only to go back two, three or four generations to find relatives who were victims and relatives who were perpetrators. Deep down, we each carry the same potential—a truth we do not like to acknowledge though we cannot honestly deny it.

I see different options for exploring the events of 9/11 depending on the person's proximity to the catastrophe. Someone may have lost a member of his family or a dear friend. Then that death is the central happening. The person who died must be seen and his death accepted. Or somebody is confronted as a political leader with the event. Maybe he wants, by means of a constellation, to find an adequate response. We could set up an organizational constellation to reflect the dynamics between the victims, perpetrators and politicians, in order to reach a deeper understanding.

Perhaps somebody is just shocked by the terrorist action, without a personal relationship to the victims or perpetrators. I see two options: 1) The person may look to the family and to the events of his own life to discover the situation(s) with which the current shock is related. Often a shocking event can rekindle a trauma which happened previously, but has been repressed. For example, a mother and father experience terror in the Second World War. Their child adopts the energy of these feelings and with 9/11, they become alive again. Or we can go still further, and perhaps find roots of the terror very far back in the past. If this is the case, it is wise to look first in the direction of the family of origin and deal with the terror that may have been experienced there; and 2) The second possibility is simply to see what happened, without prejudice or judgment. The actions and the results may seem bigger than the capacity of our understanding or compassion. How can anyone cope adequately with such an event!

In constellations, we have discovered the power and meaning that honoring brings, in particular, the honor expressed with a bow. The only right response for us in facing an event such as 9/11 is a bow. "I bow before what happened here. With this bow I do not judge. Instead, I acknowledge the limitation of my connection with what happened, without compassion, condemnation or judgment."

Bowing is not approval. It serves to separate, with respect, the one who bows from the ones who acted and leaves the consequences to them. By doing this, I become separate, standing on my own two feet and I start to see my own suffering, my own pain, my own guilt. To fully acknowledge a perpetrator is only possible if I acknowledge the perpetrator in myself, this shadow everyone carries. I leave death to the victims as their fate and at the same time, I leave guilt to the perpetrators as part of their fate. And I am connected with both, as a human being, through the bow.

Summary

In conclusion, I would like to summarize with the e-mail of an American colleague, Annie Block Pearl, from New York: "At this time, I do believe that the Family Constellation approach can be quite necessary and healing, for those who are open to its messages. I think the challenge for us practitioners here in the US is the following: we are a nation of immigrants and our national psychology has been that of independence and personal freedom. Often our ancestors left behind pain and suffering to provide themselves and their progeny with new beginnings and opportunities. Therefore, we are often disconnected from our history and our roots and perhaps are "loyal" to our ancestors and what they chose to leave behind. It is so often shocking to my workshop participants when the ancestral entanglements that are limiting them in their lives today are revealed. I think our function is as educators, and in this, we must be patient. But patience is also not in our national psyche!"

FIVE

Understanding How Family Constellations Work

The first time someone is present at a family constellation workshop, he usually is astonished to find that he can't help becoming emotionally involved in it. He or she is touched by the events which take place in the constellation, whether he wants to be or not. Nevertheless, many questions as to what's behind the family constellations remain unanswered.

The "Knowing Field"

Family constellations use something completely new— something which until now has not been consciously perceived in any other type of therapy. It is a phenomenon called the "Knowing Field"—a concept introduced by Albrecht Mahr. The work with family constellations cannot be fully grasped without an understanding of this phenomenon.

What is meant by the "Knowing Field" is that the representatives of the family members have access to knowledge or feelings of the person in the family whom they represent. They perceive feelings and relationship dynamics as the person they represent does. The representatives come in contact with a deeper level of truth regarding these relationships, when they step into the field of the family system. This is something which to this day is an inexplicable phenomenon.

The person who sets up his family members listens with rapt attention to what the representatives say. Only rarely have I had the experience that the information given by the representatives was rejected as inaccurate. Rather, there is astonishment about the truth of the representative's commentary, even when the family member's usual way of relating looks different to those who see them on the outside. In a constellation, complete strangers become a channel for the truth in the respective family and their system, as unbelievable as this may sound.

Imagine that you are taking part in a family constellation workshop. A participant whom you do not know is chosen to set up her family. She chooses you to be a representative of a family member and stands you at a certain spot in the center of the group of attendees.

As the representatives for other family members take their places and "feel their way" into their roles, your legs start shaking. You feel affection toward your "sister" standing across from you and a dislike of your "brother" standing next to you. Then an aunt who had been shut out of the family and forgotten is set up across from you. Suddenly, you get tears in your eyes and feel a great love for this person unknown to you.

It sounds crazy and indeed, it is so unusual that it is understandable if a person is skeptical at first. Common sense goes against the reality. Doubts seem appropriate. Even the skeptic, though, will see with their own eyes the representatives having reactions and experiencing strong emotions or physical sensations.

Is it the therapist's control over the group which provokes or encourages such reactions from the representatives? "Pure manipulation!" was the angry accusation I once received after a demonstration.

Or perhaps it is all about autosuggestion and the representatives bring in their own feelings toward their own families and then become steadily more involved with those feelings. No. Frequently, reactions occur which have little or nothing to do with the representative's own family.

> During the constellation for a participant with whom I felt no emotional connection, I was set up to represent her husband. Then she set up her previous husband. Even at the time she took the representative by the hand and sought out a place for him to stand, I felt an enormous anger rise up inside me. When he stood behind me and I turned around, these surprisingly strong feelings still remained.
>
> When I stated my feelings, the participant's response confirmed them, "My new husband is indeed very jealous of my ex-husband."

Common sense and personal experience are our most important frame of reference when sizing up the world. For most people, family constellations do not fit into their understanding of the world. Interestingly enough, it is often easier for lay people than psychiatric professionals to accept the phenomenon which shows itself in constellations. A psychological authority who has not yet experienced the phenomenon has a much more difficult time accepting it. His education and knowledge get in the way of his unbiased observation and assimilation of this unfamiliar phenomenon.

Let us look to physics, considered to be more straightforward and tangible, for a comparison.

> When two elemental particles crash into each other in the same way that billiard balls do and then fly in different directions, it can happen that they stay connected to each other in a long-lasting and puzzling way. From then on, whatever happens to one particle seems to directly influence the other particle through a form of telepathy. Using these principals, physics researchers at the University of Innsbruck, Austria, were able to extinguish light particles in a type of sender, in order to resurrect them in the same moment in a receiver a few meters away. The most bizarre thing about it is that the distance between the sender and the receiver plays no role. The mysterious particle transport would succeed even if the sender was stationed on Earth and the receiver was at the other end of the Milky Way. (*Der Spiegel*, I 98)

Compared to such mysterious phenomena as this, family constellations seem to work simply and transparently. Even if it makes us feel vulnerable, it may be that we simply have to accept the fact that phenomena occur in our world which we cannot (yet?) explain. The Knowing Field is one such phenomenon.

For those who are understandably cautious, observing this work, or—even better—taking part in it, is recommended. Personal experience is the best proof. While it may seem difficult the first time a person participates as a representative, one gets used to the phenomenon with each successive representation until the "Knowing Field" finally becomes familiar and practically taken for granted.

The "Knowing Field" does not only appear during Hellinger-style family constellations, but also in other settings as well. Here is an example from a theater exercise in which I took part.

> A participant who had troubles with his father was challenged to a role-playing exercise. He chose a fellow actor to play his father and set him up on the stage. Suddenly, something occurred to the participant, and he said, "By the way, my father lost a leg in the war. But I can't remember which one it was." The actor called back [correctly] from the stage, "I think it was his right leg."

Because of my ongoing work with family constellations, I had gotten used to representatives experiencing the physical sensations of the people they represent. Surprisingly, there was no further doubt voiced by the others present during similar brief role-plays in the acting course.

This observation brought me to the conclusion that the same "Knowing Field" may also appear in other forms of therapy. The psychodrama specialist Grete Leutz remarked on the appearance of this phenomenon in psychodramas: "The completely spontaneous psychodramatic acting in the role of an unknown other is so true to the actual life circumstances, states of mind and reactions of that person, that it is hard to believe that the psychodrama "actor" has no knowledge of the person they are playing." Thus, the "Knowing Field" appears in other contexts as well. Only there, it hasn't been given the attention it deserves.

The energy of "the Knowing Field" expresses itself in two different ways. In the first way, family constellations are a type of revelation of the underlying energies present in the family. This is shown by the position of the representatives relative to one another, both in distance and in the direction in which they face. The representatives feel these energies and communicate them to the group.

At the same time, the "Knowing Field" contains an energy which strives towards healing. The representatives feel "pulled" in a certain direction, sometimes strongly, sometimes weakly. This pull may move in the direction of either the problem or the solution. The therapist is able to trust that the representative's movements reflect the feelings of the person they are representing, and his or her experience will assist in discerning the possible step(s) towards a good solution.

This is shown in a new type of family constellation which Bert Hellinger often uses, in which only two people are represented in the constellation:

> The daughter had many difficulties with her mother. She sets up a representative for her mother and one for herself, placing them far apart from each other. They look in opposite directions. The challenge for the representatives given by Hellinger is this, "Center yourself in your roles and follow your impulse as to which way to move, without saying a word."
>
> The daughter and mother stand still for almost two minutes before the first movement is cautiously made. The mother turns slowly toward her daughter. Another minute passes before the daughter cautiously turns around. Very slowly and hesitantly, the daughter takes a couple steps toward the mother.

> The mother, too, then takes a step toward the daughter. Finally, they are standing in front of each other and they then look at each other as if they were seeing each other for the first time. Afraid, the daughter takes one more step in the direction of the mother, who opens her arms and then holds her child.

Sometimes this type of process stalls and the therapist must step in and either suggest certain movements, or bring the constellation back to the original type of constellation, proposing statements for the representatives to say.

During his work with constellations, the therapist learns to trust the "Knowing Field" more and more, "hear" its messages and let himself be guided by it. Sometimes it leads to astonishing experiences. It is as if a force-field emerges which was unleashed by the person who set up the constellation. Here is an example from a seminar which was facilitated by a colleague and myself:

> A participant states that her issue is her strained relationship with her thirteen year-old daughter. The mother has a secret: she doesn't actually know who the daughter's father is, although she told the daughter that she did and named the father as well. When she was asked how many men come into question, the mother said, "Ten." She was in Asia at the time and for a short period apparently completely cut loose, sleeping with ten different men. Despite using protection, she became pregnant.
>
> The woman, her daughter and the named father were all set up. There were some pleasant feelings between the father and the daughter. We decided to set up the other nine possible fathers as well. The mother noted at this time that there were an additional two men who could be the child's father also.

> I was standing by the daughter's representative and was completely surprised as she whispered to me spontaneously "he's the one" as the second of these last two men was set up. With everyone watching, she went without hesitation to this man and welcomed him gladly. It was as if the two of them had been reunited.

There exists the temptation to derive facts from a family constellation. However, the therapist or client who attempts to do this is treading on thin ice. A family constellation is never a reliable test of fact, for example, who the father of a child is, regardless of whether one might like to believe so, after seeing such a constellation as this one. Family constellations are not appropriate for determining facts. One of my participants reported something which makes this clear:

> In her first family constellation, a woman had received a clear sign that the man married to her mother—whom she believed to be her father—was not really her father. In addition, another man was set up, to whom her representative took a complete liking.
>
> The woman could not let go of the results of the constellation and the knowing feeling that the man she believed to be her father was not really her father. Her mother was already dead, but her father was still alive and she asked him to have a blood test to prove that he was her real father. The result: he was her father. He told her, however, that her mother had had several lovers around the time of her pregnancy and that he himself had always had doubts about whether or not he was truly the father.

Family constellations reliably show *energies* which exist within a family system, but it is essential to keep facts and the constellation energies separate. Here is another example which was reported to me by my colleague Sneh Victoria Schnabel:

> In one participant's constellation, the representative clearly had the feeling that she had been abused by the father. The father's representative confirmed this as well. However, the participant said after the constellation, that she had never been abused.
>
> Two weeks later, my colleague received a call from that participant. The participant had visited her sister and had told her about the constellation. Suddenly, the sister broke down crying and confessed that *she* had been abused by their father.

From this, one could conclude that the energy of child abuse was present in the system but that this energy had been perceived by the wrong representative—namely, the sister who had *not* been abused. These examples show how important it is to be cautious, and resist making claims about facts of the family's history that seem to be "revealed" by the constellation. Such claims are irresponsible and dangerous, and can confuse clients and be emotionally harmful to them.

I remember once getting a call from a participant about a week after a seminar. She said that she was completely confused, because the "facts" shown by her family constellation completely differed from the family in which she had grown up. My response to her was this: when there is a discrepancy between the experienced reality and a family constellation, always believe the experienced reality! We need to learn how to differentiate between facts and energetic images. If we become confused by a contradiction between the reality and the constellation, it makes sense at first to investigate the reality. If the discrepancy remains inexplicable, then it is important to stay with the known facts and reality as the accurate image.

For the therapist, it is at times a tough tight-rope walk between the interpreting the constellation energy and making careless speculation. For example, a son stands beside his mother and there is a certain erotic tension between them. After many years of experience with family constellations, the interpretation of the therapist may be that the mother had an earlier love, who the son now represents. However, the son, who set up the constellation, knows nothing of a former love of his mother's. Should the therapist set up a representative for this possible previous boyfriend? Or should he refrain from doing so because of a lack of factual evidence? If he were to set up a representative for such a man, it is possible that the feelings of the representatives already standing will not change when the man is included in the constellation. Then the representative can be removed. Such tests are possible when the result is accepted.

Another constellation from one of my seminars shows the difference between reality and the images in the family constellation and demonstrates clearly that a constellation is not a predictor of future events:

> The couple, engaged to be married in 3 months, set up a constellation. Each of them sets up their two or three previous partners, clears up old problems and gives the former partners a place in their hearts. Then the espoused man and woman turn towards one another and smile. To others, it looks as good as a fairy tale. If only every couple could be so well-prepared for each other before marriage!
>
> Two months later I get a call. The wedding has been called off, the engagement broken and the former bride-to-be is pregnant by another man.

Readers with analytic minds will look for ways to explain the phenomenon of the "Knowing Field." Is it, for example, a prerequisite that the client touches the representatives and directs them to their places on the floor? Not necessarily, because once the first representatives have been set up, the therapist can set up additional representatives at any time, touching them or not. It is enough if the therapist chooses someone as a representative, tells them where to stand and says, "You are the mother who died early." Suddenly, that representative has access to the feelings of the person they represent and immediately, the other family members react to this new person.

> During a constellation which was led by Bert Hellinger—and in which I took part as a representative—the client, who had no previous experience setting up family constellations, set up the whole family in a simple circle. Hellinger then asked the representatives to seek out places for ourselves according to what we were feeling. I felt, very clearly, an energy which seemed to pull me a bit outward, away from the circle, until I found the spot which was right for me.

It becomes even more mysterious. To check their work, therapists can set up a client's family without the client even being present. In my advanced training classes, I have experienced—with astonishment—that it makes no difference if the client is there or not. The room is filled with the same intensity as with a family constellation in the presence of the client.

The term "morphic field", has come to be used by those involved with family constellations through the work of the well-known British biologist and author Rupert Sheldrake. After experiencing constellation work, Sheldrake himself met with Hellinger to discuss this phenomenon from the perspective of their different experiences of it. Morphic field as a term is used by some biologists to describe, for example, why arms and legs are shaped differently although they have the same genetic and protein makeup. A morphic field is like an invisible blueprint according to which a developing organism or a pattern of activity assumes shape. It is a type of field which contains a kind of cumulative memory. Over time its influence strengthens and its expression becomes increasingly habitual.

However, this concept does not entirely explain the phenomenon of the unusual perceptive abilities of the representatives during a constellation. Hellinger says simply, "I see that it is there and so I use it. I leave the mystery a mystery."

I believe that for those involved in family constellations, the term "Knowing Field", scientific or not, most accurately describes the phenomenon seen in this work.

The Role of the Representative

Representing is an essential part of the work with family constellations. But why does one need representatives to begin with? Aren't they just substitutes for the real family who doesn't choose to be present? Wouldn't it be better if the actual family members represented themselves in the constellation?

Experience with family constellations shows that the answer is "no". This is because representatives have a big advantage over the real people. They are unbiased. That is why the client—who *is* present—chooses a representative for himself as well. The client holds all of his own memories of his family, gathered as a child, a youth and an adult. The result is that the client has attitudes and beliefs about his family which have solidified, despite more recent or additional information available to him. That is why, for example, the real or perceived lack of attention from his parents when he was a child, is as painful now as when he first experienced it. The old accusations and blame remain alive and influential.

The client—any one of us—clings to the old images of the family and defends them against change. Shifts that occur between family members in the constellation, facilitated by statements suggested by the facilitator, possibly even come about too quickly for the client to take in. The old images are, at first, stronger than the new perspectives.

Representatives by definition do not have such ingrained feelings about the family members, who are usually unknown to them. That's why access to "the Knowing Field" is possible for them. In contrast to the family members themselves, they are in a better position to sense the energies present at the moment. They are flexible and follow the changes as they become aware of them, without attachment to any previous feelings.

For the therapist also, it is easier to work with representatives than with the actual family members themselves. Sometimes the client himself cannot at first comprehend the shifts experienced by the representatives. At the beginning of the constellation, he relives the old tensions he is familiar with in his family. Ten minutes later, a deep awareness and feeling of love has emerged between the parents and the child. Ten minutes, though adequate for the representatives, is often too fast for the client. He needs more time to assimilate the new image.

Sometimes the following occurs: After an hour-long family constellation, peace comes over the family. Difficult obstacles have been overcome along the way and the therapist, as well as the seminar participants, feels a sense of relief. Then the client takes the place of his representative at this concluding stage of the constellation. He is suddenly filled with anger and tension, which seem to burst out of him—feelings which did not show themselves in this intensity during any part of the constellation. Then the constellation may continue a while longer with the client himself.

The representatives know only the essential facts about the family. The client is discouraged from talking about things which go beyond fact, such as dynamics that he attributes to family members. The representatives know nothing about the feelings of the family members or about their relationships with each other. Also, any instructions from the client about the place the representatives take and the direction they face are forbidden. He is not allowed to sculpt or create postures for the representatives (e.g., having someone kneel or point), direct their gaze (e.g., "You must look downward"), dictate their movements (e.g., "You move from one parent to the other") or suggest their feelings (e.g., "You feel sad").

Because the instructions for the representatives are minimal, they are able to expose themselves to the unknown, which they experience from their respective places in an objective way. They are like receptacles through which the energies of those whom they represent flow. Their job is to perceive these energies and communicate them, when asked, to the therapist. They often experience strong feelings, which change as they are experienced. Communicating their feelings to another representative without emotion, or at times just to the therapist is often enough for a shift to occur. That is why the representatives in family constellations take on a special role in service to others. In this way, a distance is maintained from what happens, for all those involved. Again and again, constellations approach the form of a ritual. In the old Greek tragedies, the actors wore masks through which they spoke. Perhaps these old Greek tragedies had a similar effect on the people watching them that family constellations have today.

Aside from his role serving others, the representative also has a "filtering" function. She is closest to what is felt in the family and can feel in her own body whether a certain statement or intervention has an effect or not. When in doubt, the representative is usually right, regardless of whether or not it is convenient for the therapist.

When someone watches a family constellation for the first time, he often questions whether or not he himself is capable of being a representative. Experience shows that in principle, everyone is capable of it. It is not necessary for the representative to be especially sensitive, imaginative, or have any "extrasensory" or psychic capabilities.

The representations that people take on have their own power, so that anyone who enters that representation perceives similar feelings. Sometimes reactions are colored by the people who fill the role, so that, for example, one person may experience feelings in a dramatic way, whereas someone else's feelings are more contained. Sometimes the person choosing a representative knows about these individual qualities and then chooses according to which characteristics they feel are needed for the role. In general, representatives gain experience with each role they have, becoming more and more able to contain strong emotions without dramatic responses.

The concern that a representative's own personal feelings and experiences are mixed in with those of the person he is representing is almost never borne out—even if the representatives are chosen according to their own past histories. For example, there may be a participant who is always chosen as a father or another who is always chosen as the younger sister. If a participant takes, for example, the role of a younger sister in a constellation and she is indeed a younger sister in real life, she may have doubts at the start of the constellation as to whether or not her feelings belong to the family of the client or to her own family. However, those who have been representatives repeatedly learn to trust their feelings as representatives. When feelings emerge, they (almost) always belong to the role one has taken in the family being represented. If a representative becomes flooded with his own personal memories of his family—something which is, according to my experience, very rare—then the therapist and the other representatives are able to notice this and the representative can be replaced. The therapist can also ensure that someone is not put in the same role (e.g., that of a youngest brother) too often.

Can representatives be manipulated? Is it possible for the therapist to influence the representatives according to his own ideas? Hardly, for even those who take a role for the first time can feel whether or not the sentences proposed or the places he is moved to cause him to feel better or worse. As long as the therapist trusts the responses of the representatives, manipulation from him or her is unlikely.

One enters dangerous waters, though, when the therapist looks for a certain answer or uses "loaded" questions. For example, an acquaintance once told me about a time when she was a representative for a daughter who was standing across from the father. She had the odd feeling that the father was somewhat foreign to her, which she mentioned.

The therapist then asked, "Is this man even your father?" This question brought her out of touch with her feelings and made her feel very insecure. In that moment it would have been possible for her to agree with the therapist's notion and reject the man as being her father.

Even though every representative is an instrument in "the Knowing Field," there are still various depths and levels of accuracy which emerge on an individual basis. Representing people who are unknown, trains a person's ability to perceive these foreign energies and also refines it. Experienced representatives can feel the feelings and energies very accurately and give very precise information about them.

The Use of Language

Those who get involved with the work of Bert Hellinger and family constellations come into contact with words and sentences which seem at first strange and somewhat foreign, such as, "Dear father, I honor you." The language almost sounds like it comes from the Middle Ages or as if it carries religious overtones. It is no wonder that a person's first impression of family constellations is that they have stepped into an ancient, conservative or antiquated world. Colleagues of mine who now work with family constellations have told me that they would throw Bert Hellinger's books at the wall the first time they read them.

Only those who choose to take part in family constellations or get deeply involved in the written material can see why such words and phrases are used and the healing impact that they have. The words perfectly convey what needs to be expressed. It is a simple, almost archaic manner of speech:

"Dear aunt, please give me your blessing when I live on." Or, "I honor your death and your fate." What sounds like old-fashioned formality has a directness which fits effectively in the context of family constellations. Through these words, we come into contact with a fundamental level of emotion which lives in each one of us.

These statements, strengthen, release and reconcile. After saying them, the representatives stand straighter, or they exhale in relief, or they look at others in a friendlier way. The statements are chosen with this outcome in mind, and they are judged by whether or not they achieve this positive result. What counts in the constellations is the effect they have—an effect that is visible in the posture, on the faces and in the breathing of the representatives.

Bert Hellinger discovered these sentences in the same empirical way, by observing and noting the effect they had in the constellations. Everyone who observes a process in order to evaluate it must likewise recognize and put aside any preconceived notions and ideas. Anyone who observes attentively is able to recognize which sentences are effective in bringing peace and reconciliation to a family system. What must be avoided is choosing sentences according to whether or not they fit into a preconceived ideology or world view, or according to an outcome which may be desired or forced.

These sentences are naturally concise. As such, they cannot be further modified, and there is no need to make them more palatable. They may seem almost ritual in form. However, it is important to keep in mind that all rituals run the risk of becoming superficial when used automatically and mechanically. Therefore, these simple but potent statements, developed by Bert Hellinger, will also lose their effectiveness if they are used mechanically as a routinized technique or magic formula. The full effect of these sentences unfolds only if they are accurate, i.e., when they truly reflect the representative's feelings, the atmosphere of the exchange and the current situation in the family.

In addition, the therapist must be in contact with the client and the rest of the group as well as staying connected to "the Knowing Field." Otherwise, the therapist is like a parrot that repeats Hellinger's sentences from a handbook, as if they were a one-size-fits-all remedy for any family conflict. Fortunately, the representatives perform a corrective function, as they can most effectively determine whether or not a proposed sentence is accurate and appropriate in the moment.

As with other psychological methods, over time, a unique language has developed, among those involved with family constellations. The jargon used in the constellations is the "Hellinger language" which stems from Hellinger's books and seminars. Some clients even come to me self-diagnosed: "I am entangled with my mother and I wish to give it all back." I personally recommend that one moderate the use of the language developed in the constellations and confine it to the context of family constellations, rather than using it in general conversation, thereby diluting its effectiveness.

Aside from the completely descriptive form of the "classic," almost ritual statements used, for example, to resolve issues between parents and children, there are other types of sentences used in family constellations as well. One type is sentences which reveal and shed light on tensions that exist in the family.

A husband is placed facing his wife. He knits his brow and starts making fists with both hands. The therapist proposes that he say, "I am angry with you."

> The man says the sentence and immediately exhales
> deeply. "Yes, this sentence fits," says husband. He felt
> relieved after saying it. The wife, too, feels relieved.
> "Finally it is out," she says to the therapist. Then the
> therapist proposes the sentence "I feel very hurt by
> you." The man repeats it and finds that this sentence
> is also accurate. He feels good saying it.

With each of these sentences, another level of feeling is
addressed. When anger is acknowledged, then feelings of
hurt and pain emerge. The important thing, is that even
strong emotions are not shouted out cathartically, but rather
are expressed with simple words and short phrases stated
calmly by the representatives. When something is discovered, it is as if the sentences which resolve problems emerge
on their own. Then they are fresh and correspond specifically
to the situation. Again, the *effect* of the sentence proposed is
what determines if that step was fruitful.

In addition, there are simple sentences which objectively
reflect reality. Sometimes the representatives in a family constellation are confused. No one seems to know who belongs
to which generation, who is a parent and who is a child. Even
when they stand in the final order, they don't recognize each
other. In such situations, it is sometimes enough to propose
and repeat straightforward sentences which simply name the
reality, such as, "I am your father, you are my son," or "I am
your wife, you are my husband and these are our children."
These sentences have power because they explain the situation. Saying them creates order in the confusion and helps
each individual to relax in their roles.

Sometimes there is no confusion, but rather the reality
itself is very unpleasant or alarming. Especially at this time,
it is important to have the representatives state the facts.

Even the most shocking situations or experiences lose some of their disturbing effect when they are simply named. It is the job of the therapist to expose the shocking experiences. Here is an example from a seminar in which a participant's mother had killed her disabled daughter and then killed herself: I proposed that the representative for the mother say to her disabled daughter, "I am your mother and first I slit your throat, then I killed myself." Sometimes, as was here the case, the resistance to stating such a reality is enormous. When it is done, however, the relief experienced is equally enormous.

I have had good experiences in difficult situations when formulating statements for representatives which reveal the naked truth. For example, there was a time when a daughter stood before the mother and refused to say the sentence, "You are my mother." The mother says to her then, "You came into the world from my womb." Suddenly, the daughter's resistance to seeing reality is alleviated.

A therapist who proposes sentences that are inaccurate is often corrected by the representatives. The observer is able to see that even inexperienced representatives rarely allow themselves to be manipulated. If the therapist finds a fitting sentence straightaway, then the representative repeats it without resistance. Paradoxically, the more experienced the therapist, the more he is accused of manipulation from mistrusting observers.

Love and Presumption

A comment from Bert Hellinger cuts to the core of the work with family constellations: "What happens through love and is maintained by love can only be dismantled through love." Therefore, children carry certain energies and entanglements from the family, out of love.

However, the surface looks much different. I like to compare family constellations to certain deserts—on the surface they may appear to be hot, dry places where little seems to grow except for thistles and cacti. Similar to the process of the constellation, we dig into the ground in search of water. At some point we find some—sometimes after just a few inches and sometimes only after we have dug, with much effort, a few feet down. When we finally hit water, it flows easily up to the surface, sometimes even rushing up like a geyser. Even though the area looked parched and barren when we started, we realize that there were seeds all around, which then grew with the water's help and the area is seen in its reality, blossoming with life.

Deep down, in every family, as disturbed as it may seem from the outside, we find a well of strength which serves life. As evil as a person may seem to have been throughout the course of his life, we often find that bad deeds spring from invisible unrealized bonds with his ancestors. These bonds come from love and the person in question is trying to help his family by carrying the burden of these problems, out of love.

Entanglements can only be resolved when a loving bond is consciously experienced as a base—not when anger and disdain is embraced. For example, "I moved across the country to get away from my parents." Or, "No matter how far away I move, my parents continue to dominate my life." What one tries to get rid of in anger returns through the back door. Anger works like a rubber band. The more tension used to hold it at bay, the harder it springs back when released.

The love which bonds a child to his family is immense, far greater than the anger that many focus on. A child would not hesitate to give his life, if that is what is required by the family. Every facet of his being wants to belong to that family. That is why he shares the fate of other family members and helps carry their pain. Because of that, however, the child does not see the other family member's love. The child only feels the pain of the other and wants to show his loyalty by melding with and imitating him, in effect impersonating the loved one.

Constellations where the mother died in childbirth show this childish—blind—love very clearly. Such a death burdens a family for several generations. For the child born to the mother who died, the burden is the strongest—almost unbearable—because he was the "cause" of the mother's death. The daughters of a woman who died giving birth are often afraid to have children of their own. The father of the child feels guilty as well, as though his sexuality "killed" the woman.

> A child stands in a constellation at some distance from his mother. He does not feel that he can look at her. As the therapist leads the child to the mother, he can hardly look the mother in the eye, because of the guilt he feels. The mother, however, looks at the child with joy and deep love. Healing and change come when the child stands before the mother, bows deeply to her, and says, "You died at my birth. I thank you for my life and I accept it at this price." The mother then says to the child, "It is the risk I accept as a mother and I carry it. It is my death and I carry it. Do something good with your life, to honor me, so that my death is not in vain." Suddenly, the child is able to look up, feel and accept the love of the mother, and also feel gratitude rather than disabling guilt and grief.

The mother gave her life during the birth of the child. If the child does not want to live, then the mother's sacrifice was for nothing. That is why the mother wants her child to lead a good, fulfilled life. When the child honors the mother and her fate, he discovers the mother's love. He gratefully accepts the mother's sacrifice and makes the best of life on her account. The blind, childish love, possible when the child looks only at himself, changes into a mature, conscious, enlightened love—a love of the "other".

With this more mature love, a person is able to see the other person and his fate and is able to honor both. The respectful bow is the ideal way to honor a person. Through the bow, a certain distance between the two people is brought about, showing them as separate people with a bond on an adult level.

With this adult form of love, a person is alone—separate—to a certain degree. He is an individual with his own life and his own fate. That is why the bond induced by a child's "blind" love seems easier to bear. It is like an umbilical cord. One fears death when separated from it. This step is also accompanied by a sense of guilt, because a person "frees" himself from another in a certain way and leaves that other person alone as well.

Adult love is something that matures slowly. Sometimes, just feeling the deep, childish love is an important level to reach during a family constellation. For someone who felt deserted by or hostile towards their parents for their whole life, the discovery of the love for their parents is in and of itself a healing step which brings them closer to the parents. It is a first step, and further movement towards growth and maturity will develop at a pace right for that person.

Childish love is one side of the coin. But turned over, we find something different:

Marc leads a very taxing life due to the number of responsibilities and obligations he takes on. After his immediate family is set up, Marc was found standing behind his father. The father feels weak and Marc has the feeling that he must support him.

An important event in the family was the death of the father's father when the father was seven years old. The paternal grandfather is then set up behind the father and Marc is placed facing his father. Marc's father is drawn to his own father, turns around, looks at him and starts to cry. His father (paternal grandfather) takes him (Marc's father) in his arms and holds him for some time.

Marc's father then turns back towards his son again. The therapist proposes that the son say, "I take my place as the child now. I am only the child, and no more." The son feels that the sentence is inaccurate and refuses to say it. The therapist then proposes another sentence, "It would be presumptuous of me to help carry this because I am only the child." The son agrees with this sentence, says it to the father and the constellation is then concluded, with some relief experienced.

Although he was a child, Marc had in a sense represented his grandfather in the family and taken on certain fates and responsibilities from him. In our work we constantly discover that when a person loses a parent at a young age, one of his or her children takes on the role of the deceased parent. This burdens and overwhelms the child, but—out of love—the child "accepts" the role. Later, as an adult, the child takes on additional burdens and permanently impairs his own chances for happiness.

The other side of love is presumption. Taking on a role or helping to carry problems inflates the child's importance.

It gives him or her more "weight" within the family. By carrying this burden, the child feels important and without it, he fears his worth is diminished. That's why it is very difficult for Marc to let go of this burden. Deep inside, he needs time to let go, to become "smaller". When grasping or clinging to a problem is revealed in a constellation and there are no signs of it shifting, it is best then to end the constellation. Simply exposing the problem provides enough impetus for change.

The following example makes the concept of presumption easy to understand: After a harsh argument between the parents, the small daughter goes to the father to comfort him. Secretly, she feels herself to be a better partner for the father than the mother is. The child then feels bigger and more important, even if she is painfully burdened with this task which is truly beyond her.

When a child takes on a fate that is not her own, but rather that of one of her ancestors, she is being, in the words of Bert Hellinger, presumptuous. This is because she is taking over something which has nothing to do with her and does not "belong" to her. It is, so to speak, "none of her business." It is not hers to take on. Every person must carry his or her fate alone, regardless of its severity. No one is entitled to get involved with it. Nevertheless, we all take on the fates of others, which is presumptuous of us, regardless of it being done unknowingly and out of love.

Perhaps the root of this lies in what we call the "ego." We build ourselves up to be something more than we are. The more a person lets go of theses fates not belonging to him, the more he is able to find the simple, innocent child within, and just live his own life.

SIX

Using the Family Constellation as a Method of Therapy

This chapter expands on the knowledge of family constellations gained from the preceding chapters. The effects of the constellations vary and the ways of dealing with those effects vary as well. There are significant differences between constellation work and other therapeutic styles and procedures. When a person experiences this work for the first time, he doesn't yet have a clear picture of it and it can be somewhat confusing.

The Effect of Family Constellations

Family Constellations have been shown to have a strong effect on the client. Here is one client's response to a question about how her life changed since she set up her family constellation three months earlier:

> Decisions are becoming clearer and their conse-
> quences are as well. Honor and dignity in a relation-
> ship have a higher relative importance. The rebellious
> view I had regarding everything "old" has made way
> for respect, though I can still see mistakes. I accept
> my role as a mother more and more with love,
> whereas I used see it as something which needed to
> be taken on with grim determination.

What are we to make of the effects of the family constellation? What actually happens during the family constellation?
We all hold an inner image of our family in our minds. This
explains why a person is able to set up a constellation of his
family which reflects an accurate representation for him. Until
the person sets up a family constellation, this image is hidden
within his mind. It is an image, not a diagram with a logical
assembly. The image does not have to be understood or justified. In the constellation, the inner image is externalized.

In a family constellation, the unconscious image of the
family is made conscious by bringing it out in the open and
bringing it to life through the representatives. The family is
brought onto the stage through the representatives and the
client then becomes an observer of his own inner image.
Excitement and tension surfaces, which until now, was hidden
within the subconscious.

Lets take the hypothetical example of a client who has
felt confused his whole life by inexplicable suffering and emotional pain. Secretly, he has even wondered if he is crazy.
During the family constellation, he sees with his own eyes
that his representative experiences the same confusion. It
then becomes clear to him that these feelings are not inherent in his personality, but rather stem from his relationships
with his family. They have to do with the place that he holds

within his family, because anyone else who stands in his place within the family and takes his role (i.e. represents him) feels the same confusion. Discovering this does not change his feelings, but the burden begins to feel lighter when its effects are physically seen. He gets a certain distance from his feelings and that also provides some relief.

As I mentioned before: when tensions are simply talked about among family members, they change. That makes room for something new to happen. Sometimes a family constellation is like a drama which exposes the anger, guilt and entanglements that exist within a family. They appear, enlighten us, dissolve and change us. The love which had been hidden until then is able to surface.

In this way, the constellation, as well as the image that it reflects, becomes more relaxed and peaceful. Deep down, the client discovers a deep connection with and love for his family. One can imagine the client carrying this peaceful image with him into the future and one can see how much more relaxed and compassionate the client feels with that image.

At the end of the constellation, the client may be brought into it, standing in the place where her representative stood. Although she is still an observer of the constellation, she is also taking part in it. The entire time, she had been observing the process from a distance and now she joins the system in its new order, feeling what it is like to be in a new position relative to her other family members. This has a greater emotional impact on the client than if she were to simply observe the constellation the entire time. The client becomes a part of the constellation and perceives the other representatives as if they were the actual family members.

In order to strengthen the experience, the therapist may propose sentences for the client to repeat, such as "Dear mother, I am your child. Thank you for giving me life." The therapist must find a good balance at this point, because for some clients, the insight gained from simply observing the family from the new position is enough, whereas others need additional means to experience and feel.

As mentioned earlier, the process with the representatives is easier than with the actual family members because the representatives are able to take in and evaluate the effects of the sentences and changed positions in an objective, unbiased way. The therapist should also ask himself if he is making the work more difficult by bringing the client in at a certain point and whether or not it is really necessary for the client to experience the constellation himself.

At the end of a constellation, the client's job is easy. He holds the new image of his family in his mind and lets its healing effect unfold, without actively doing a thing. Understanding or analyzing this image is not important or even beneficial. It is an image which works of its own accord. Just as the old image previously influenced and directed the client unconsciously, the new image will work in the same way.

However, for most people, seeing it manifested before them is something completely new. We are used to working out problems in our minds. Our minds engage automatically and can be difficult to stop. Our minds strive to understand, and *now*! Questions start shooting through our minds immediately. "What is my family constellation trying to tell me?" "What am I supposed to make of it?" "Should I call my mother today and talk about this?" "Or perhaps write my father a letter first?" These thoughts can provoke such a strong storm that the image is almost blown away. An example from one of my seminars illustrates this point:

> The client had a brother who died young. She encounters him in her family constellation. Love starts to flow when he says, "It is my death and I carry it. You honor me when you let me own it. You are only my sister."
>
> Later, during a conversation, the client mentions offhandedly, "I knew I was incompetent." Taken aback by her remark, the other person asked, "What do you mean by that?" She answered, "Well, that's what my brother told me in my constellation."

The client was convinced that she was generally an incompetent and incapable person. Such a conviction acts like a filter, allowing in only those thoughts and ideas which support it. In this case, the meaning of a statement had been twisted and stretched until it fit her belief about herself. To her, the fact that her brother took on his own death, meant to her, "You are unable to carry it, you have done a bad job of it." The true message of the statement, as well as her brother's love, didn't reach her—the filter prevented that from happening.

Experiences like this shake us awake, because up to this point, trust in the power of the constellation image had been enough. What is a person to do when the filter is so strong that the new information cannot get through?

Perhaps it is time to give more attention to a response known by other types of therapy as "resistance." The fact that some inner walls are built high and seem at first insurmountable, is something which has rarely been addressed by those doing family constellations. Allowing a healing image to take effect requires a certain discipline of the mind, which is considered inaccessible for the unpracticed. For me, the fact that these new images have a fair amount of impact on the client *in spite of* inner barriers, shows the power of family constellations.

So that the client has time to let the new image of his family sink in, there is an unwritten rule which states that a participant should not be a representative in a constellation directly after he has set up his own constellation. Also, he should be shielded from questions asked by other participants about his work or his feelings. This is a spiritual process, a process which operates on the soul level, and the person needs time and space to let the image unfold. That is why there is no discussion or interpretation of a constellation right after it. That would bring our analytical minds back into play, which would hinder the new image from taking effect on the nonverbal level.

However, to prevent misunderstanding, it is important to note that what happens in a family constellation is not a set of instructions for action. A person who takes action based on his family constellation directly after he experienced it has probably not recognized this fact. Sometimes it takes months for the change born of the new inner image to show itself in a natural way through a person's actions or behavior.

Often confusion and doubt arise in the hours, days or weeks after a person's family constellation. A person has a certain image of his family that he has carried with him for his whole life. All of the tension he experiences and the wounds he has nursed are contained in that image. For many people, that image may be incomplete and one-sided, but there are real reasons for that. The new image shown in the family constellation is a truer picture of the family, an image in which love flows between parents and children. Previously, the client had rarely if ever experienced such a view of his family or even thought it possible. Therefore a part of him resists the new image, preferring the familiar comfort of the old.

It is important to know that these phases of confusion are common and it is best to allow them. To trust the new image and its power and possibility is the most helpful inner attitude to hold. For a client who tends to analyze and brood, the facilitator may recommend that they just forget the image seen during the family constellation all together.

Family constellations give the soul a push, so to speak, in the right direction. They are about personal growth and personal growth cannot be "produced" using some kind of technique. The less the push comes from the therapist, the more that growth is in the hands of the client. The client takes more responsibility this way and is more empowered. Hellinger describes this process as "minimalism," which means that the therapist does the least possible.

When the therapist finds the point where the most energy in the system is tied up, one option is to stop there. At that point, enough of an impetus for change has been given and that energy then can be used by the client for personal growth. If the therapist works beyond this point, the energy could diminish or fizzle out altogether. For example, a client feels very lonely and has no relationship to her parents. In her family constellation, she reconciles with her mother. Her mother takes her in her arms and holds her a long time. Such an encounter needs time to unfold. The power for this unfolding is lessened if one were to work on the client's relationship with her father immediately afterward, just for the sake of reaching reconciliation there, too.

For client and therapist alike, it is helpful to take the attitude that the effect of the family constellation is not in their control. It is not a type of work which can be performed in a goal-oriented way. The result unfolds on its own.

The Role of the Therapist

Those who observe a family constellation for the first time and are familiar with other types of therapy, are often astonished that the therapist acts with such authority. He gives a client sentences to say and edits them according to his discretion. He moves representatives to different places in the room seemingly at random, and he brings in only those ancestors that he determines relevant. Sometimes the therapist even refuses to have a client set up his family because his issue is not yet clear.

This is all fairly unusual and differs significantly from the actions of therapists in other types of therapy. Are family constellations then, the therapy of choice for clients who look to an authority figure to tell them what to do? Must a person who facilitates family constellations have an authoritative personality?

Family constellations are led with authority. The danger does exist that over-zealous therapists, able to imitate yet inexperienced, can take on an authoritarian tone without truly being prepared for the responsibility. The choice of words, strict tone of voice or gruff manner is not what matters. The most important prerequisite for this work is the therapist's ability to sense the "Knowing Field" and be connected to his own intuition.

Before I became involved with family constellations, I had worked for many years with Neuro-Linguistic Programming, a method of therapy in which the therapist's awareness of and response to the client plays a central role. Authority with the client is neither used nor expressed. At that time in my life, I felt somewhat uncomfortable or out of my element with authority and had no desire to take an authoritative position.

The experience of facilitating family constellations brought surprises for me. In some situations, the authority and confidence to lead the constellation would simply come to me. I was so sure of what I perceived that I could take the risk of directing with a certain amount of power. This type of confidence in my directive abilities was new to me. The more familiar I became with this work, the stronger I felt this sense of certainty and sureness. This sense of confidence in my ability was not something which always accompanied me, but rather it was like a guest which liked to visit me and did so more and more often.

I suspect that it is the power of the "Knowing Field" which cultivates the necessary authority and certainty in the therapist. A person who exposes himself to the "Knowing Field" is opening himself to change. He becomes more sure of himself and gains access to his inner feelings and intuitions. To me, this is the reason that family constellations became so popular in Germany—and not just with clients, but with therapists as well.

The authority is not an end in and of itself—it is only one side of the coin. The other side of the coin is that the therapist learns to follow the energy of "the Knowing Field" as it passes through the representatives. Only when the therapist is in good contact with the representatives and trusts their reactions can a family constellation unfold.

There are other dimensions to which the therapist attends as well. I see the work with constellations as a balance between three different aspects. These aspects are: the energy shown by the representative, the orders in a family system and reality.

Energy

Reality   Order

The therapist works on one of these aspects at a time, but is always aware of the other two aspects in the background. He brings them into play one after the other in varying order, all the while paying close attention to the responses and impulses of the representatives. The more experience he has, the more his perception of these movements is honed. For example, a son bows to the father, and the therapist notices that the father wrinkles his forehead. Or perhaps an aunt who died young is added to the constellation and her niece exhales audibly. The therapist notices these responses and addresses them, either through an inquiry (e.g., "What just happened for you?" to the representative, or "What happened with your father's father" to the client) or by proposing new statements to the representatives (e.g., "Tell her, 'I'm so glad to see you, my dear aunt'").

The more the therapist notices, the fewer questions he has to ask the representatives, because he can see which way the representatives' energies are going. Also, the representatives have the best sense of what is going on in the family. The therapist observes the representatives' reactions and can trust them. He is guided by their behavior; they show him whether he is on the right track or not. The quality of his work is measured by how much he works according to the representative's responses. The representatives' "trustworthiness" (i.e. the validity of their access to the "Knowing Field") is displayed by the previously mentioned constellation type where only two people take part and no sentences are proposed. In this type of constellation, the representatives follow their inner impulses and intuitions derived from the "Knowing

Field". They show the hidden workings of a family system and are often able to find a solution on their own.

The orders of a family system form another aspect—which is almost directly opposite to the energy in a constellation. These orders have been confirmed in constellations over and over again. And, exceptions to these orders have also been confirmed. That is why there is no hard and fast rule regarding the "correct" order in any respective constellation. The therapist must use all of his knowledge about rules *and* exceptions to find a good order in which all of the representatives feel well. Repeatedly, the therapist's interventions are drawn from the orders which rule the majority of families.

Finally, it is also important to include the aspect of reality. Reality includes the facts about the family that the client knows and tells. Often the therapist must bring these facts into play. For example, a client reports that her father sexually abused her. At first there is nothing in the family constellation which reflects this fact or makes it otherwise visible. The client's representative looks happily at her father, who stands facing her in a peaceful way. In order to introduce reality, the therapist proposes that the client's representative say "You abused me." An important element of reality has then been brought in, the feelings of the representatives change and the therapist can proceed with the new situation.

Finally, there is the "spotlight", the decision about what exactly will be looked at in the family. First and foremost is the client. The family constellation is set up for her and it is for her that a solution is sought. All conflicts, tensions and entanglements which do not involve the client are not addressed, as they would only distract from the issue. If the client has an especially important issue, then the "spotlight" is used to illuminate the darkest corners of that issue.

The aspects of energy and order influence the style of an individual therapist the most. There are those who focus on order. As a result, the therapist leads the representatives as quickly as possible to the places which correspond most often to a good order. The sentences which he proposes are oriented towards and emphasize order. The danger with this type of order-oriented outlook is that the therapist might not pay enough attention to the responses of the representatives. He becomes inflexible then and it is possible for him to overlook many of the family dynamics as they come to light. He hesitates when an exception to a rule is seen in the constellation and is not sure how to proceed. He can then become defensive and try to "force" a solution by applying the rules he knows, which in this case might not fit.

Then there are therapists who first and foremost let themselves be guided by the representatives' energies. This type of therapist trusts that the order which springs from these energies is the best one and he concentrates completely on the representatives. However, when he flows exclusively with the energies of the representatives, he is in danger of getting caught up in that flow and being carried away. At some point, then, the family constellation stops making progress and the representatives simply get caught in their roles. It is necessary to use reality and order as points of reference. Each aspect gives clarity to the constellation, but neither one of them alone can result in resolution.

In fewer cases are those therapists who rely only on reality, which limits the possibilities open to him through the family constellation. Order, as well as the representatives' reactions, gives the therapist clues as to which direction leads towards resolution. A therapist works most effectively when he uses all of the aspects available—reality, energy and order.

In the trainings I offer, the model of the triangle "Energy—Order—Reality" has proven itself to be very helpful when analyzing mistakes made in the work. When a family constellation is full of problems and mistakes while lacking in solutions, it helps to find out which of these three poles has been neglected and which has been overemphasized.

From my point of view, therapists are able to develop and improve most when they follow the energy of the constellation, the "Knowing Field". Of course, as a prerequisite one needs sufficient knowledge about family constellations as well as the ability to bring in reality and order. However, these aspects are limited in their scope and also fairly easy to grasp. The most significant and incalculable part of a family constellation is its energy. The more the therapist trusts the energy, the more he is able to enter the unknown.

Bert Hellinger has emphasized the importance of a therapist working without intention—without attachment to a preconceived outcome. This includes the intention to help or heal, as well as the intention to change fate. What does he mean by that?

In my work, I differentiate between two types of intention. On the one side, I obviously wish and intend to help clients find a path towards healing though the use of the family constellations. I experience this intent like a natural river that runs through the constellation. Difficulties and problems continually occur. I first try to overcome these and sometimes it works out. Sometimes, though, the river seems to come to an abrupt end. If at that point I keep working with the constellation, out of stubbornness, fear, pride or the "need" to heal, then I have the second type of intention, fueled by my own agenda, which is dangerous to the welfare of the client. Working without intent inevitably yields the most fruitful result.

Therapy or Life Help?

Family constellations are a method of therapy in their own right, though the full extent of the inherent rules and limitations has yet to be ascertained. How do we know that family constellation work can even be called "therapy"?

That question logically leads us to the next: What is health and what is illness? There is no clear line between the two. Let us take, for example, a person with feelings of dissatisfaction and sadness which gradually becomes stronger and more frequent. Finally, it takes up all of his energy and emotional paralysis may overcome him.

At what point along the spectrum does the person go from healthy to sick? First we have the inner, subjective criteria that a person feels sick, weak and vulnerable. Above and beyond that, there are the objective symptoms which designate whether or not one is sick—such as being bed-ridden, difficulty coping with every-day life, or being declared sick by a doctor or other medical professional. Nowadays we find a lot of criteria and definitions defined by law—something necessary for insurance purposes. Strict definitions are needed so that health insurance is not abused.

Beyond that, the term illness leads us to the areas of career and class politics—determining who is well-educated enough to address difficult types of illness, who should be allowed to do this type of work and who should not. Given the flood of doctors, psychologists, alternative healers, social workers and life coaches in practice today, it is mostly about the ability of the workers in each respective career field to earn a living.

The question as to whether or not family constellations are a type of therapy, according to legal criteria, so far means little to the family constellation facilitator. That is because legalities mean little in terms of the essence of the work. From this perspective, it doesn't matter if a psychological disturbance is large or small, whether it is about mild or severe depression or thoughts of suicide. The focus is on the systemic causes, causes which stem from entanglements with the family of origin and sometimes also with the present family system.

Since 1995, Bert Hellinger has led seminars in which he demonstrates his work in front of hundreds (on occasions even thousands) of therapists and doctors. Often, the clients setting up their families in these seminars suffer from severe illnesses—from cancers of all types to other physical diseases, from psychosis to schizophrenia. It has been shown that there is no fundamental difference between working with these clients and working with people who have less severe, more "normal" problems, problems that many of us face (sadness, depression, work or relationship difficulties). In the procedure as well as in the solution, the severity of the illness or problem is irrelevant.

From the paragraphs above, one can derive the answer to the question of whether or not constellation work is a type of therapy. Simply put, the answer is that it is a type of therapy when used as a treatment for illness. It can have a deep impact on the illness and contribute to healing. A therapist needs more knowledge and skill to master difficult situations—those involving ill clients—because the condition of the client is often easily influenced. A person with a degree in medicine or psychology, however, should be qualified to carry out this work with people who are in such conditions.

Setting up a family is not a type of therapy if the client is not sick. This includes most people who attend the family constellation seminars. They have the everyday problems and difficulties that come with living life. Family constellations help them with their problems and have a "reconciling" effect. Unknown contexts become visible. Fundamental orders become understandable. That is why many therapists offer constellations to the general public. Today, family constellations are reaching a broader spectrum of the public than any other previous type of therapy. As is usually the case, women are the first to come and men lag somewhat behind. It is clear, though, that most seminar participants are not "therapy junkies" who follow every new therapeutic or esoteric trend. They are married and single mothers and fathers and single people without children. They are a cross-section of the population.

Here is a typical example from my circle of friends. A daughter in her mid-thirties borrowed a video about family constellations from me and watched it with her mother during a weekend visit. The mother was so impressed, that she paid for seminars for all of her daughters as well as for one daughter's fiancé. She did not take part in a seminar herself, however, claiming that she was too old for such things. Three months after her daughters' seminar, she and her acquaintance of the same age signed up for one of my seminars.

Is a Family Constellation a One Time Event?

How many family constellations should a person set up in order to explore her family? During the early years of his work with family constellations, Bert Hellinger went strictly by the rule that every person should only be allowed to set up their family of origin once and their present family once. He thought that setting up each system one time should be enough for a good effect to unfold, as long as the person had faith in the results of the constellation. Hellinger believed at that time that a person who wanted to set up his family a second time did not trust his own soul and was therefore not accomplishing anything positive. He believed that the only legitimate reason to set up a family twice was if new, previously unknown facts about the family history had since come to light. Only this would justify setting up another constellation of the same system.

Since then, however, opinions have changed. An important turning point came during the first convention of the Association of Family Constellation Therapists in Wiesloch, Germany, 1997, when Bert Hellinger took the podium. He claimed that his position had changed, and that the first family constellation that a person sets up reaches only the first level of a person's personality. He believed that there were deeper levels of the personality and deeper entanglements which could be reached by setting up additional family constellations.

To me, a comparison can be made here with the discovery of fire. When humans first discovered fire, their fear and respect must have been enormous. With time, they learned to control fire to a certain degree. Then fire slowly became more familiar to them, and with caution they began to use it as a means towards certain ends. Today children are taught about fire; they are taught that they should respect it and that they should not play with matches, for example.

To me, this is comparable to family constellations. As the existence of the "Knowing Field" was discovered and experienced in the constellations and its power made visible, the awe of this phenomenon was enormous. Meanwhile, we have lived with the existence, knowledge and durability of "the Knowing Field," for more than a decade now, and it is starting to become more familiar to us. Now we can start, with the appropriate caution and respect, to further explore its possibilities.

I, too, have come to see repeated participation in family constellations over a lengthy period as a valuable tool which furthers personal growth. Someone who thinks after one seminar that there is nothing more to be gained has not recognized the potential of family constellations. It has been seen that participants who have set up their families multiple times are continuing a process and expanding their understanding. Also, being an observer or a representative, as opposed to setting up your own family each time, has been shown to have value as well.

My own experiences have been most convincing. After setting up my family of origin, changes came quickly and fundamentally and they were clear and impressive. However—and this is to be expected—I also experienced a lot of inner conflict and blocks. I dealt with these issues for a long time—sometimes in small, private groups and sometimes alone. I discovered that deep down, these issues had hidden themselves within the many facets of my life and the family constellations were helpful in increasing my understanding of them. (I sometimes suspect that this is why I have such an interest in this work—because I have found a way to keep working on myself with this process).

In the seminars which I facilitate, I have experienced that insights can deepen even when a person does another constellation only two or three days after the previous one. Often, on the last day of the seminar, there is time for post-constellation work, which means there is an opportunity for some participants, depending on the time available, to look at a specific aspect of their constellation in more depth. This is done with the help of a very short constellation of no more than ten minutes in length.

Recently, a father came to a family constellation seminar wanting to resolve his relationship with his youngest child— a 19 year old son. On the first day, he set up his present family system—his wife and children. The constellation revealed that there were several entanglements which especially had to do with the oldest child. There was no particular focus on the youngest child and in the family constellation there seemed to be no problems associated with him. On the last day, the father requested some post-constellation work. This time he set up only himself and his youngest son. An enormous tension between the father and son was found. The son was afraid of the father, because he sensed an anger in him— an anger of which the father was not aware. It was shown that this anger of the father had been taken over by the son. Only when the father was prepared to own his feelings of anger, could peace return to the relationship between the two. This short constellation went much deeper than that of the first day and brought much more clarity.

It takes time for the inner image of a constellation to take effect. When someone requests a second constellation, the answer to one question is pivotal to me. That question is, "Does this person wish to dig deeper and understand more?" Only when the answer is "yes" does it make sense to set up another constellation. On the other hand, perhaps the person wants to set up another constellation because he doesn't accept what was shown in the first constellation, or is resisting the outcome of the first constellation. Perhaps a client says something like, "What my constellation showed me was terrible. I'd like to try it again." This clearly shows that the client hopes to invalidate the first constellation because he didn't like the outcome. Doing a second constellation in this case serves no purpose and would be in vain.

The deciding factor is whether or not the first constellation showed something real, regardless of how undesirable or frightening that result is judged to be. The important thing is to confront this inner image and to work with it. That is not always easy. Indeed it is sometimes painful, even excruciating. It can take a long time—sometimes years—for such images to become integrated into a person's consciousness.

I believe it shows positive progress that there are more and more training and advanced training courses available in family constellations as time goes on. Family constellations have "tools of the trade," too, and it is advantageous to be able to try out and practice these tools in a safe environment. Aside from that, the training courses offer an opportunity for long-term personal growth. In the courses which I lead, I enjoy watching how participants become more sensitive representatives and how the themes and issues of their family constellations cut more and more to the core. Things which were unclear and hidden at the beginning become clear and explicit with time.

Can Family Constellations Be Dangerous?

A person who leads family constellations as a form of therapy should be aware of their potential dangers. I remember the case of a therapist who was taking part in a family constellation seminar put on by a therapists' association.

The therapist's issue was her difficult relationship with men. When telling her history, she mentioned that she had been abused by her father as a child. She had already addressed and worked on that issue during ten years of personal therapy. On the first day, she set up her family. The topic of abuse seemed to be mostly resolved.

On the next day, harsh abuse was again the theme in the constellation of a fellow participant. The abuse had been so bad that the parents had given away their rights as parents and the resolution for this client was to turn away from her parents.

Later that evening, I ran into the therapist on the street. She was crying so hard and was so confused, I could hardly speak with her. She told me, stammering, that the other woman's constellation on abuse brought back the full pain of her own abuse. It took quite a while for her to calm down and return to her "normal" self.

The next day, we set up her family again and this time the abuse was portrayed as being much worse than in the first constellation. It was so bad that the most suitable solution in her situation was also for her and her parents to be left turned away from each other.

Occasionally, family constellations unleash enormous energies. Feelings hidden under heavy guard can break through to the surface all at once. This is not always predictable, as was the case in this example. If a therapist, even one whose intentions are good, puts the constellation to use in a careless or naive way, there is a danger that the power of a constellation can grow to a point where it can no longer be controlled.

It is important, then, to know of a protective framework for possible complications in a constellation. Often, family constellations are carried out in seminars. The participants come together for two to six days, set up their families, stand as representatives in the constellation of others and then go their separate ways. In most cases, the client comes to the seminar alone, and is often alone with his experiences afterwards—experiences that he must deal with as best he can. Participants frequently experience strong feelings after their constellation seminars. What would be a possible safety net for the participants?

One possibility is for a client to include family constellations in a larger framework of ongoing therapy with another therapist. The patient then has a person with whom he can talk about his experience with his family constellation. For instance, therapists who are familiar with my work, send their clients to my seminars. After the seminars, these clients return to their personal therapists and are well taken care of.

Complications can also arise, however, when the client's therapist is unfamiliar with family constellations. In this case, the therapist understands neither the concept of "entanglements" nor how constellations work. This simply puts an additional burden on the client. My recommendation to clients, who find themselves in difficult life circumstances, is to seek additional support from a therapist who is familiar with family constellation work. A constellation affects a deep level of the personality and a client may need support afterward.

Another concern about family constellations is whether or not diving into the roles of strangers can be dangerous for the representatives. Can the average participant tolerate the tension that some roles generate? It has been shown, for example, that a representative, who took on the role of a family member who was heavily burdened emotionally and whose tensions were not released during the constellations, carries those tensions in him for a certain length of time after the constellation is over. It is then the therapist's responsibility to help the representative consciously step out of his role and leave it behind. I have had some good experiences with clients directly releasing the representatives from the roles they took in their constellation. One way is for the client to look at the representatives and say "I gave you the roles of my family members. Thank you for representing them. I now take them back."

There are other occurrences which remind therapists to use caution and gentleness. I remember a constellation in which the client was entangled with the deaths and harsh fates of several family members. I had just turned to one of the uncles when something hit me in the back. The client's representative, who was actually an experienced representative, had just fainted and fallen on me before hitting the ground. Fortunately, she was not injured. She immediately regained consciousness and stood up. Since that time, I often ask someone to stand behind a representative who is in a difficult role in the constellation so that they can be supported in case they lose their balance or fall.

Experienced representatives gradually become more and more impervious to these foreign energies, though it takes time before a "green" representative can do this. For a person who is especially sensitive or impressionable, a particularly difficult role—for example that of a handicapped child who was killed in a Third Reich euthanasia program—can be too much of a burden. The therapist should be aware of this and take it into consideration, perhaps choosing a more experienced representative for such a role.

Another experience I had also showed me the potential dangers of family constellations. In one of the advanced training courses that I led with my wife, we did some post constellation work for a client at the end of the seminar. The client, represented by my wife, was being irresistibly pulled towards death. No intervention I made could change that. Finally, I had to accept this end result, as well as my limitations as a therapist. It was very difficult for my wife to come out of the role afterwards. She described her feelings in the role as being a terribly cold void that she was helpless against. She needed almost one half hour of movement and walking before she came fully back to her normal self.

I was not able to let go of that experience and while reading one of Bert Hellinger's books, an idea for a new type of intervention came to me. When the course met the next time, I decided to try my idea. The same representatives took their roles and I tried the idea, but it did not help. The pull Death had on the woman remained uninterrupted. After five minutes, I ended the constellation.

My wife's terrible feeling of cold emptiness, though, had intensified, becoming almost unbearable. The energy of another person had practically become a traumatic experience in its own right. This feeling slowly disappeared, but it sometimes returned at night while my wife was lying in bed. It would take an hour of therapeutic work to get the feelings to completely subside. This fate from another person had become so powerful, that for her to take on this role a third time would have been completely irresponsible.

Examples like this show how important it is to be alert and prudent. Arrogance or overconfidence with this work can put us in positions where we no longer have control.

What is an Individual Family Constellation Like?

The work with family constellations is evolving. Originally, family constellations were only carried out with the aid of representatives. It was soon discovered that a group is not always needed to perform a family constellation. In individual therapeutic situations, family constellations are carried out in a different way. For many clients, it takes an enormous amount of courage simply to go to a therapist and to speak about their problems. Some people are afraid or uncomfortable with sharing their problems in front of a group. For them, it would be too much of a burden to participate in a seminar which lasts several days.

Thus, therapists have been able to modify the family constellation procedure in such a way that it, or at least the essential core of it, can be carried out by two people. In order to do this, two aspects of the constellation are changed—the space where it is held and the method of representation. This type of individual therapy has more similarities to Gestalt therapy and psychodrama methods than the seminars do.

Since only the therapist and client are present in this type of individual therapy, objects are used for representatives. In the simplest variation, cones or blocks are placed on top of a table to represent family members. Each relevant person in the family is set up and the direction they are facing is also determined. After a short time, the client has set up a family constellation using the cones. As incredible as it sounds, a "Knowing Field" in which the two persons present take part, emerges here as well. In other words, knowledge about the family in question is suddenly accessible through the pieces set up on the table.

That's why the next step—that the therapist or client can "feel their way into" the roles of the various family members—is possible. Looking at the cones, the therapist can then ask the client, for example, "How would the father feel in this position?" That is a big difference from the group seminars where the client sits and observes from the side and only at the end slips into his own role. The therapist himself may also slip into the roles of the family members and communicate his perceptions from each respective role. One after they other, the feelings of all the family members who have been set up are revealed.

Despite the small space of a table, insights are gained from individual sessions just as in the usual family constellations. This process, however, does require a fair amount of abstract thinking in order to comprehend some things. Thus, there are several variations of this type of constellation in which the room itself is brought more into play. In this case, cushions, shoes, books, mats or pieces of paper with names written on them are used.

To start, the therapist at first represents the respective family member and is set up by the client. Then the object (e.g., shoes) is placed there and the therapist steps out of that role and is then set up in the next role. If the therapist or client wishes to feel their way into a certain role, they can do that by standing at the respective place where that person is represented. Naturally, a fair amount of flexibility, sensitivity and experience helps one to go from role to role. Another option is for the therapist to take over the different roles as representative while the client simply takes note of his own reactions.

> The client stands at his place in the constellation. The therapist goes to the mother's place and

stands in her role. He pays attention to the feelings he gets in that role and communicates them to the client. "I don't feel any love for you," he says. The client feels the feelings that this sentence releases for him. The therapist leaves the role of the mother, comes to the client and proposes the sentence, "Even if you do not feel any love for me, you are still my mother and I am your son." The therapist then returns to the place of the mother, listens to the client say the proposed sentence and then pays attention to what he feels in that role. The process then continues until a resolution is found.

In this type of individual family constellation, the client has the advantage of being able to face a person instead of a cone, piece of paper or other inanimate object.

Another variant is a family constellation which is completely carried out in the mind using the power of the imagination. In the next example, Ursula Franke describes the procedure with a client who has first been brought into a relaxed state of mind.

> *Ursula:* "Imagine that you are standing in front of your mother. . . . How is she looking at you? How are you looking at her?"
>
> *Client:* "I am doing well. I am a bit sad, but it is good to see my mother."
>
> *U:* "How is your mother looking at you?"
>
> *C:* "Lovingly, tenderly, but somehow I feel that she is restless."
>
> *U:* "What happens when you stand your father next to your mother?"
>
> *C:* (The client starts to cry.) "I want out of here. I can't stand it."
>
> *U:* "How is your father looking at you?"

C: "He's not even looking at me. I can't even see him."

U: "Where is your father?"

C: "I don't know."

U: "What happens when you set him up far away from you?"

C: "I feel more calm."

U: "How does he feel over there?"

C: "He is sad and helpless. That is not where he belongs. He isn't looking at us."

U: "How do you feel when you look at him?"

C: "It hurts so bad here." (She points at her chest.) "It's so hard."

U: "What happens when you back up a bit?"

C: "I feel better." (She exhales.) "Now I can also see my mother again."

That is only the beginning of a session. Subsequently, the other family members are brought into the picture. Changes in the places they stand have an effect and sentences which the client says or hears also cause shifts to occur.

Family constellations carried out in the form of a seminar have certain advantages. The energy of "the Knowing Field" seems strongest here. There is more intensity and the feelings are clearer and more distinct. When the family system is complex, what the physical representatives communicate is helpful in understanding the network of relationships. In addition, the image of the family is more complete when one can see the entire family at the same time.

On the other hand, if there is just one person in the family that is very important to the constellation, for example, a sister who died young, then setting up a constellation of just two people can be enough. A constellation of two family members is just a first step. After that, many clients feel more prepared and willing to do a family constellation in a group setting and that is usually a noticeably more intensive, insightful and healing process.

Setting Up Feelings,
Parts of a Person's Personality and
Material Objects in Constellations

At this point, I would like to mention several other important developments in family constellations. Organizations can be set up in constellations in the same way that families can. It is an astounding fact. The principle of representation functions in the same way in this case, as it does in the family constellations. Single members of organizations or even complete departments may be represented and they perceive the feelings of those represented. Above and beyond that, there are orders to be aware of which are unique to organizations while sharing similarities with the orders in families.

Not only can families and organizations be represented. Some therapists use constellations to represent feelings and parts of the personality. The aspects of a person's personality can actually be set up with representatives and the representatives are able to provide very precise information. Tensions become visible and solutions can develop. Insa Sparrer and Matthias Varga von Kibéd have developed their own form of this work with precise guidelines, calling it "Systemic Structural Constellations."

When an issue can be named with a feeling, it can help sometimes to set up that feeling in a constellation. This is often done as a first step or in preparation for a family constellation.

The client suffers from panic attacks in public. They are so strong that he avoids being out among people.

In the constellation, the client and his Fear stand back to back. At first, the client is afraid to turn around. After the therapist encourages him, he turns around slowly and cautiously. His Fear, on the other hand, has a neutral attitude, but turns as well. The client wants to have more space between them. He takes a few steps back and can then relax. Then he bows to his Fear and says to him, "I honor you. You are part of my life." The Fear feels more accepted and becomes friendlier. The client can now look at him more directly and is more comfortable in his presence.

Some of the principles of the work with family members are also important in these constellations. For example, if a person is not seen in the constellation, it is good to shift the representatives in such a way that eye contact can be made or the representatives may be moved to a more comfortable distance (i.e. further apart) instead. If a person is too close, the other representative may feel pressured or threatened by that closeness and cannot look at or see the other clearly. However, if the representative is too far away, then perhaps he cannot be looked at or seen clearly, either. The representatives can find the best distance between them. When good eye contact is made, the next step comes easy—honoring that person or, in this case, the feeling. Bowing is always an appropriate expression of respect.

Finally, it is important to recognize belonging or ownership of something. Just as every family member belongs to that family, every feeling belongs to a personality as well. Whenever a person tries to fight a feeling or suppress it, a negative inner tension is created. When a person such as this last client, refuses to accept his Fear, he gets caught in a vicious cycle. He fears his Fear and is then permanently imprisoned by this feeling. In a constellation, the client sees his Fear, honors it, accepts it and owns it. After that, he relaxes and can start to let his Fear simply be. By doing this, the Fear diminishes. Then he can begin to look for the root of this fear, which often lies in his family of origin.

Even worldly objects, such as money, can be represented. These representatives often experience strong feelings, too. Now, common sense tells us that bills and coins probably do not experience much in the way of feelings. Then where do the representative's reactions come from? These feelings are the feelings of the person who sets up the object (i.e. the client). The representatives perceive the feelings of the observer, the client. Through the use of constellations, we discover that we assign feelings to our environment and those feelings come to light through the representatives.

For some people, everyday problems become hurdles that they can't overcome. Often the reason for this emotional stress stems from the family of origin. In the next example, the client's problem was that he became extremely nervous while giving speeches and was not able to connect well with his audience.

> The client first set up himself and his Audience. He stood near the door and felt like he was being pulled out. The Audience stood behind him and wanted to hold him back, away from the door. The first move was for the client to turn around and look the Audience in the eye for the first time. The Audience was friendly and the client relaxed. Something seemed to be missing, however, and the facilitator proposed that the topic of his talk also be

set up, because after all this was what he wanted to communicate to the audience. The Topic was set up across from him and also wished him well.

Now we looked for a good ending order in which all three—the client, the Topic, and the Audience—could feel at ease. At first the Audience was set up at the side of the client and the Topic was set up across from them both, facing them. The client and the Audience were satisfied with this order, but the Topic wasn't! He was moved to the right, then to the left, with no positive change. Finally, an idea came which resolved everything. The Audience and the Topic should change places. The Topic then stood at the side of the client and the Audience stood across from them, facing them. Suddenly, all three felt at ease.

The client, who was scheduled to give a talk the next day, told me afterward, that he pictured the topic at his side as he climbed the stairs to the podium before his speech. As his speech began, he only had slight stage fright. The pressure, from which he had previously suffered, was gone.

What is the makeup of the "energy burden" from the family of origin mentioned above? I knew from the client's history and family constellation that the client was drawn towards death (manifested in the pull towards the door). The client had already encountered this inclination in a previous family constellation, and had found, at that time, an image of the family which provided a solution. As the next constellation showed, though, traces of a problem already resolved in a constellation sometimes remain in another area. The audience, in other words, his work, keeps the client alive. It is no wonder that with this tension (the pull towards death) he had little strength to make good contact with his audience.

Other constellations show the original relationship between the problem and the family as well:

> The client had already set up a constellation of a very strained family of origin. At the end of the seminar, she spoke about her fear of becoming addicted to drugs, because the father of her daughter is addicted to heroine. We then set up her and a representative for drugs. She chose a woman to represent drugs.
>
> She is looking straight ahead, with the drugs standing behind her. I recommend to them that they pay close attention to their inner impulses and follow them without speaking. For a minute, both of them stood still. The woman then slowly turned around. The drugs looked at her lovingly, and opened her arms. The woman closed her eyes and let herself be held for a long, long time.

This was a view into the depths of the subconscious, into a level of feeling which lies beneath the fear of drugs. The client finds consolation, warmth and security in drugs. Who is the person in her family that can give this to her? It would seem to be the mother. Her true search, then, is for her mother. The drugs are simply an imperfect, unhealthy substitute, which bring no healing.

I had a discussion with Bert Hellinger on the topic of constellations of feelings, aspects of one's personality and relationships to material objects. He has reservations about this type of constellation if the connection with the family is lost. From his perspective, there are relationships with family members that are hidden behind these feelings, which should be seen and honored. Hellinger believes there is a danger that a superficiality or shallowness could emerge, which will cause "the Knowing Field" to retreat.

On the day after I had this discussion, I received a letter which was a good illustration of Hellinger's reservations. An acquaintance of mine wanted to participate in one of the family constellation seminars I was giving and asked in the letter, "Do you work with the inner child or the higher self during your constellations? Can this be requested?" The special thing, the new thing, about family constellations is that they help us put our feet on the ground. They lead us to our roots by showing us how we are related to our parents and to our families. It is a long process of being confronted with and coming to terms with our families, which is not always easy. However, afterwards, a person is more securely attached by both feet in the world. A person avoids this confrontation when he sets up his "Inner Child" or his "Higher Self" instead of his family.

A question about the image of "the Knowing Field" has occurred to me. Is it a type of energy which was unknown until recently and which someday will be scientifically provable? This would be similar to the way that pyramids produce a special type of energetic field around them which can be proven, though the reasons behind it are unknown. It would mean that this field is always there—usable and at our service—independent of the topic or of our own attitude towards it. Or is it a new type of field which is connected to our "soul?" This could mean that we cannot get it under our command or that even trying to would close off our connection with it. Perhaps trying that could even be dangerous.

For example, in NLP (Neuro-Linguistic Programming), there is the so-called "Core-Transformation Process," which leads a person to inner happiness and fulfillment through a series of prescribed steps. However, people who have practiced NLP regularly have told me that with time, the effects become weaker, more diluted.

Our "soul" does not let itself be manipulated with techniques. When we try it, we are led astray. At this time, many questions remain unanswered and we can only learn from experience.

Constellations as Life Training

Family constellations bring us in contact with a new reality. Still, there are certain principles used in constellations which can be used in everyday life as well. That is why I call participation in this type of work "Life Training." It shows us the actions and attitudes needed to have a more fulfilled life.

No man is an island. The first important lesson that one learns in family constellations is that we are all connected. From insights we gain, feelings emerge which can change us.

> In a constellation, a client stands across from his mother and father, but feels cut off and lonely. When he looks his father (who grew up without a father) in the eye, he sees that his father also has the same feeling of being cut off and lonely. The grandfather, who committed suicide at a relatively young age, is then set up. He, too, feels cut off and alone. Suddenly, the client realizes that he is bonded to the father and grandfather through this feeling of loneliness and of being cut off. In fact, this feeling creates the bond.

Experiencing such a bond nourishes and relaxes the client in a deep way. When a person has been involved with family constellations for a long time, something fascinating happens. That person starts arranging old family photos on a table or wall in some part of the house. Suddenly, that person has much more interest in the dusty, old family photos.

Why is that? A person who has a photo of the grandparents or great-grandparents on the wall recognizes that he belongs to that family, that he is a part of it. He discovers that he is part of a greater whole. He is born, grows up, perhaps has children himself, grows old and at some point dies. This is how it was for those who came before him in the family and this is how it will be for those who come after him. He experiences himself as part of this continuity. Many things are put into perspective. For example, the importance of beauty, attractiveness and youth. One sees in the photos that life comes, stays for a time and then leaves.

A certain sense of peace emerges from this connection that we have with the family, as well as a sense of trust in the life which flows through the generations. Also, because of this sense of connection, we are more able to accept what *is*. There is a feeling of life taking you by the hand, even if you cannot completely understand it, because life is much larger than our ideas about who we are and what we want.

A basic respect for other people comes from discovering this connection. It becomes apparent that all other people are also connected to their family in the same way that you are with yours. In family constellation seminars in which everyone sets up his own family, judgments and prejudices against the other participants disappear in a surprising way. When a participant, even a pushy, disagreeable one, sets up his family, the feelings he carries and the ways that his actions are connected to his family becomes visible. A deep understanding emerges and our previous judgments or prejudices seem arrogant and superfluous. One learns to accept people the way they are.

In the constellations, bowing is a way of most clearly expressing respect. The experiences that participants have when they bow to each other, even just during an exercise, are quite enlightening. The most important thing is that the bow be genuine, not acted. The representative being bowed to can tell immediately if it is genuine or not. Some representatives are surprised to find that they do not feel smaller than or inferior to the other when they bow. In fact they feel better, as opposed to their experience of being forced to "bow" to the parents that some experience as children. However, the person being bowed to does not feel superior to the person bowing either, but rather feels respect towards that person as well.

Marianne Franke-Gricksch, an elementary and middle school teacher in Germany, describes how she discussed a question with 11 to 13 year old students about the effects of gestures. The topic was respect as well as giving thanks, by putting one's hands together and bowing, something that Turkish and Indian children are quite familiar with. Each morning several children, who represented all the children in the class, bowed slightly to their classmates. A noticeable atmosphere of respect unfolded in the classroom. An example which Ms. Franke-Gricksch gave on the topic of community and belonging was also impressive:

> "I once had a student who would interrupt German and Ethics class, kick other children in the shins and only rarely complete his homework, although he was a talented child. Soon it was too much for everyone in the class and the class speakers wanted to talk about it. They wanted to put him on the "hot seat" and tell him about everything he does which angers them. I refused and asked them for one more day of patience.

On the next day at the beginning of class, I called the problematic student to the front of the class. I told him that we all had something that we wanted to say to him, the same thing from all of us. I started and said to him, 'Rainer, you belong to us.' Twenty-two children then proceeded to tell him the same thing. When the last one was finished, a great silence filled the classroom. We were familiar with this type of silence. It is the type of silence that occurs when something genuine is about to happen. Rainer cried and then quietly sat down in his seat.

We never talked any more about it. The boy used this opportunity, and in the next few weeks changed his behavior."

Another important element in this life training is to increase awareness of your own responsibility. That is not an easy thing to do. Secretly, we often believe ourselves to be innocent in conflicts and arguments. We prefer to see ourselves in the role of the victim instead of that of the perpetrator. Then, as innocent people, we become very angry at the people who committed an injustice against us.

The client had lived with her boyfriend for three years and she then became pregnant. She knew that her boyfriend wanted no children under any circumstances. Out of fear of losing him, she arranged to have an abortion. She insisted, though, that the boyfriend accompany her during the abortion. One month later, he fell deeply in love with another woman and left her.

During her constellation, she felt a huge, dark, all-consuming hatred for her ex-boyfriend. She accused him of not wanting the child. Nothing seemed to be able to penetrate her hatred. I then proposed this sentence to her, "I take my responsibility

for the abortion and leave you to take your responsibility." With those words, it seemed as if she suddenly
woke up. Her cold hatred changed into anger and
underneath the anger, her pain could be found.

The client had put the entire blame and responsibility
for the abortion on her ex-boyfriend and had not seen her
own part in it. When she became aware of this, her approach
and attitude fundamentally changed. Family constellations
make it possible for people to see their own part in a situation. It brings things into focus, makes them clearer. Then we
are able to see both sides—the other person's mistakes as
well as our own.

In the end, family constellations show us the power of
facts—the power of reality. Our lives are often ruled by the
belief that our thoughts and intentions are what counts. For
us, such things count more than what we have actually done.

A person who has good intentions but does something
bad or evil against his will considers himself to be innocent.
Thus, there are "pseudo-resistance fighters" who take part in
the atrocities of a harsh regime, while all the time feeling
innocent because they did so reluctantly and therefore, deep
down, are innocent.

Family constellations help us to recognize that we are
responsible for our actions and for the result of those actions,
regardless of what kind of inner justifications we hide behind.
A person can drink himself senseless and then kill someone
while "legally incapacitated" or "of unsound mind." However,
family constellations show that a person's subconscious does
not excuse them. A person must still carry his guilt and
responsibility for the death of the other person. Our vision of
reality is no longer obstructed by our ideas or thoughts of

who we are. It stands there before us, clear and simple, diminishing pretense and promoting authenticity.

However, the reverse is also true. Often people feel guilty because they had bad intentions, even if their intentions were never carried out.

> A client sets up her family. Her mother did not want her and during her pregnancy had often considered having an abortion, but at the end, let it be and had the child. The mother feels very guilty facing her daughter and has problems looking her in the eye.
>
> Then the mother says to her, "I wanted to abort you, but I didn't do it and instead brought you into the world." This simple sentence relieves her feelings of guilt and allows her to look at her child lovingly.

Facts have their own special power. To look the *facts* in the eye, rather than nurturing our *ideas* about the facts, makes life less ambiguous and helps make us stronger.

At the same time, one discovers more power when one puts facts and feelings into a few, simple words. The representatives don't get caught up in the emotion of the role, but rather just state the essentials in a short sentence, such as: "I am angry with you. I blame you for . . . (etc.)" Astonishingly, doing this in everyday life, too, often has a better effect than an emotional outburst. Marianne Franke-Gricksch gives an example from her school:

> "Saying 'I'm sorry,' coupled with a small bow has a deep effect in regards to solving conflicts. Even the children recognized that the phrase 'excuse me' is not enough.
>
> "The question as to whether or not a person should use such symbolic actions, moves the children.

They found out that one's actions, body language and a concise sentence is enough to do something effective—especially when it is followed by an earnest 'I want to make it up to you.' Otherwise the children give long justifications to their parents, teachers and friends.

"The children started to practice in this way and had a lot to report. They were proud when they were able to re-establish an emotional equilibrium with a concise sentence and respectful actions. They also noticed that true intentions must be behind the actions and statements; otherwise, they don't work. The children increasingly took pleasure in trying it out. They even developed a standard procedure for times when they came late to class. They would come to the podium at the front of the class, bow slightly and say, 'I am sorry.' Often we had to laugh, because we could tell it wasn't true. But then the ice had been broken and we could look for a more suitable sentence, for example, 'It was not important for me to come to class on time today,' or, 'It would be better for me to make an excuse, because I am actually not yet sorry.'"

Beyond that, family constellations impart life experience. When a person represents someone unknown, the client comes into contact with the unfamiliar. When a young woman has the experience of being a great-grandmother, proud of all of her children, grandchildren and great-grandchildren, then she is able to experience this feeling 60 years before she normally would. When a hard-core bachelor stands in the role of a father, filled with pride when he looks at his children, he is experiencing something new and important.

Along with that, there are difficult, extreme roles, for example, that of an SS soldier or a Jewish person in the Third Reich. The experience of a woman, who, due to a lack of men in the seminar, took on the role of a man, also fits into this category. Her role was that of an uncle who had sexually abused the client. Afterwards, she told of the experience of sudden strong sexual arousal, an experience new to her. Such roles lead people through human highs and lows. The representatives gain insight to which they would not normally have access. The roles also lead one into his own personal depths and impart an existential understanding of other people and their fates.

SEVEN

The Various Possible Uses
of Family Constellations

The chapters up to this point have dealt with the background of family constellations as well as how they work. In this chapter, we will explore some new areas. The possible uses of family constellations go much further than those mentioned up to this point. Their potential is tremendous. In some respects, this work has just begun and it is not yet possible to see all of the directions in which it will lead.

Family Constellations in Prisons
and with Criminal Offenders

Crime and criminals are becoming a focal point of modern society. Statistics show that violence is increasing in many segments of the population, especially among children and youths. Enormous problems are coming to light, which are being discussed at length in the press. What are the causes of this recent development? It seems to be a multi-faceted problem. And society's efforts to control it thus far have been largely unsuccessful.

In researching the causes of crime, there are two essential questions: (1.) Why would someone from a normal, middle-class household become a criminal? And (2.) Why do some former prisoners return to crime, becoming repeat offenders? The current issue of sex offenders is a good example of the insufficient answers to such questions. Their unexplainable, at times gruesome acts have shocked the public repeatedly. Occasionally the perpetrators have had a difficult childhood and—from that point of view—repeat with others the wrong which was committed with them. This is not, however, true in all cases. How then, do some people come to do such heinous acts?

Even explanations by therapists and psychiatrists don't seem to provide adequate answers. When asked, for example, what a perpetrator finds so stimulating about abusing and torturing children to death, the answer from one professional was, "For the perpetrator, it is about doing something new. Somewhat like being the first to tread on freshly fallen snow." The explanation from the same interview that "the pleasure which is created is simply stronger than the aversion" raises more questions than it answers. Why is there such a perverse desire in some people to begin with? The explanation that there are genetic causes seems to be an attempt to pacify in the absence of other feasible explanations.

Bert Hellinger's approach provides us with new answers to these questions. The interest in using family constellation work in corrective institutions is also growing. The practical conversion to the correctional institution environment is just at the beginning. We need to apply the orders and principles that have been discussed so far to the specifics of the offender. A prisoner is also the child of parents and a member of a family. Many causes of a punishable offense can be traced to the offender's family of origin. The causes of repeat offenses, like unavoidable fates, can often be found in the bonds with the family.

That is shown clearly by the family background of a prison inmate charged with a drug offense. With many drug addicts, a bond to a deceased person in the family can be found. They are being pulled toward the deceased and towards death and drugs are the means to that end. That is why the desire for drugs is often greater than the will to quit. The client's attitude was one of apathy, due to the amount of medicine that she required. Nevertheless, she was able to set up her family.

> The mother of the inmate was the youngest of seven children. As Gypsies, her six sisters as well as her parents were sent to a concentration camp during the Third Reich. There they were gassed. During the deportation to the camp, the client was somehow given up by one of her sisters and she survived.
>
> Her family constellation showed the mother's deep love for her family, which pulled all of them—including the daughter who survived—almost unstoppably towards death. The inmate stood there, full of pain, facing the deaths of her family members and bowed deeply before them saying, "I honor your deaths and your fate. Please be happy for me when I live on." She then felt more calm and peaceful.

In this constellation, it becomes visible how a person can feel guilty due to the bond with dead family members—survivor's guilt. The power and will to live is almost completely absent in such a person.

In family constellations, many such explanations for criminal offenses are discovered. Especially the seemingly senseless acts of youth violence often stem from the violence perpetrated by previous family members. Perhaps a great-uncle was a murderer, who is thereafter bonded to the victim. Sometimes a rage breaks out in the child—a rage that had been controlled and suppressed in the parents and other ancestors.

The peculiar thing about a feeling like rage, which has been taken over by a family member, is this: The enraged person feels as though he is in the right. Reality is somewhat nebulous to such a person. An accurate view of his actions is not possible. A person who becomes a criminal offender due to an entanglement feels innocent. The entanglement makes it difficult or impossible for him to see his own guilt. That is why regret is impossible for him to feel.

Family constellations show us directly, before our very eyes, how compelling and forceful this bond is. This blind force to imitate those who came before us visibly shows itself as stronger than the willpower to resist committing such crimes. As long as this sinister bond has not been dissolved, many perpetrators are unable to be law abiding. Falling back into criminal behavior is "pre-programmed."

Yet the work with criminal offenders shows the same mechanisms that are at work in every family. It makes these mechanisms and their particularly negative effects visible. People who have been imprisoned repeatedly have more burdened family backgrounds than "law-abiding citizens."

There are three steps which are necessary to take when working with criminal offenders. The first two steps are the same as those needed to resolve any entanglement. The first step is for the offender to recognize how his actions are related to his family. As with every other constellation, the offender must find the loving basis that connects him to his family. As one can imagine, a child who is prepared to sacrifice his life, would gladly also become a criminal if it serves the family in some way.

The first step then leads to the second step, which is to resolve or change the bond in the family that is having a negative effect. This includes honoring the fate of the person with whom one shares this bond. Then the offender leaves the ancestor's responsibility for his life and his actions to him.

The third step is to take responsibility for one's own actions. With a criminal offense, this includes being able to see one's own guilt. It is necessary for the perpetrator to be confronted with the criminal action committed in order to perceive his own guilt. More precisely, he or she needs to be confronted by the victim. Regarding sex offenders and repeat offenses, the fact is that in therapy, the actual deed—the crime—as well as the victim often remain in the background. As long as the offender does not look his victim in the eye, it remains unclear to him exactly what he has done. Only this existential encounter with the victim will give the perpetrator insight and allow regret. Although it is expected and sometimes demanded of the perpetrator who commits a crime, pleading guilty in court is often a means to avoid paying a higher penalty and is otherwise not meaningful.

On the other hand, when a perpetrator encounters his victim, it often has a positive, even healing effect. That is the basis of perpetrator—victim compensation or "Restorative Justice" as it is widely known. This has been introduced as a new type of sentence, especially among first time and juvenile offenders. In this program, the perpetrator meets with the victim and tries to make a "reparations" agreement out of court, in order to restore something of what the victim lost in the crime. The perpetrator has the opportunity to see the consequences of his actions, to see the injustice that he caused, and, as far as is possible, to contribute to a settlement.

A family constellation in which only the perpetrator and the victim are set up has similar intensity as an actual meeting between the two in real life. In fact, the effect can even be stronger and leave a more lasting impression. As we have experienced from such constellations, feelings often emerge in a very moving and powerful way. The actual perpetrator, who watches his or her constellation from the "sidelines," doesn't feel pressured to "pretend" regret for the audience. He, too, is part of the audience—an observer. In this way, he has a certain amount of inner space—a certain amount of breathing room—in which he can face what he did and work on it deep inside himself.

In this way, the constellation confronts both the perpetrator and the victim in a very direct way with the deed and its consequences, without diminishing its impact. The perpetrator's deep bond with his family becomes visible. The perpetrator is unable to dodge the responsibility for his actions, because it is there, right in front of him. An important function of being sentenced for a crime, which is coming to terms with the criminal act committed, can be achieved in this way.

The family constellations that I carried out in a prison illustrate what I have written about so far in this chapter. The offender's deep bonds with his family become visible. Here is an example of a female inmate who had been imprisoned on numerous counts of fraud and other scams.

At first, the inmate, her family and—further away—the victim of her fraud was set up. The perpetrator was not emotionally moved in any way when facing her victim. The mother had the feeling that she encouraged her daughter (the perpetrator) to cheat and engage in acts of fraud. (The inmate then stated that her mother sent her to the shopkeeper to steal when she was a little girl.) The daughter feels very connected to the mother, but her distance in the face of her victim hasn't changed

Only when the mother's mother is set up is there a shift. The granddaughter felt especially connected to the grandmother, whom she had experienced as being phony and deceitful. The mother was moved to a spot between the two. She then said, "I am the big one and I take on my guilt and responsibility. You are just the child." She added, "So that it finally stops!" Now the perpetrator at last feels free. She is able to look at the victim and say, "I am sorry."

The powerful, negative influence that a certain type of behavior can have in a family becomes clear in this case. The malevolent bond between the daughter, mother and grandmother and the resulting inner compulsion to cheat people and commit fraud, came to light and were dissolved to a degree. Only then could the inmate begin to regret her criminal offense, as well as be able to express that regret to her (represented) victim.

What kind of inner effect does it have when one accepts one's guilt in such a situation? These and other questions are posed frequently, especially in the case of murder. What is the meaning for the offender when he leaves the family and goes out the door, or when he lies beside the dead victims? Does this mean he should commit suicide? Is there no other solution than for the offender to leave his family? And what does that mean?

A family constellation, which Bert Hellinger carried out at the end of 1998 in a prison near London, England, gives us insight into what the solution might be for such heavy guilt.

> The man setting up the constellation had beaten a man to death in a bar room brawl. At the time of the constellation, he had already served twelve years of his sentence. Only the offender and the victim were set up in the constellation. I (the author) was the representative for the victim. At first, we were not able to look each other in the eye. A murderous rage rose up inside me, along with the feeling that I, too, could have killed him and that I could have been the perpetrator. The perpetrator started to sob and then knelt down, crying, to the floor. I felt sorry for him and laid my hand on his shoulder. After a time, we both looked each other in the eye and then held each other. After a time, I had the feeling that it was enough and I stood up and stepped back.

This constellation shows how guilt can be taken on by a perpetrator. The perpetrator looks the victim in the eye and he realizes what he has done. By doing this, he takes responsibility for his actions. Then, or perhaps even before that point, he feels an intense pain that he lets in completely. After some time, the pain goes away, and the strength for positive action is there. There are no short cuts through this process or ways to speed it up.

Gunthard Weber, one of the most experienced family constellation therapists and the man who represented the perpetrator, said after the constellation, that he had never felt pain like that before. The perpetrator, who had been observing the constellation, was visibly moved and said "I felt that, all these years."

Another enlightening constellation regarding the dynamics found in prison was a short organizational constellation about the residents in a reform school. The issue was that a group of youths of Kurdish heritage had shut themselves off from the German youths in the school. There were repeated outbursts of violence from the members of the Kurdish group.

One person was chosen to represent the German youths and another was chosen to represent the Kurdish youths. In order to get a complete picture of the dynamic, a person was also chosen to represent the school administration as well as another to represent the social workers, who's job it was to re-socialize the youths and further their rehabilitation.

> In the constellation, the two youth groups stood across from each other at a distance. Between the youths stood the reform school administration and the social workers, who were also facing each other. The youths looked at each other as enemies and the Germans felt superior to the Kurds and looked down on them. The reform school administrators perceived an atmosphere of suppressed violence and otherwise felt the same as the social workers, that is, weak rather than strong.

I searched for an order that would be a suitable solution in this constellation. First, I placed the Germans and the Kurds next to each other. Immediately there was a release of tension between the two groups. I then stood the school administration in the "first" place, across from the representatives of the two groups of youths. This was because the best order in families and organizations is an order in which those who are responsible for the security and well being, or ongoing progress, stand in the "first" place in the constellation. In this place, the representative of the administration was able to relax and had the impression that from here on out, the administrators would be able to work well with the social workers. The youths also felt good in this order.

The social workers took the second place, directly to the left of the school administration, also facing the youths. Contrary to the other representatives, who felt good in their places, the social workers felt decidedly bad. Their representative refused to stand beside the administration. She wanted to stand between the two groups of youths. As she took the place between them, though, a tension spread among all of the participants. I ended the constellation at that point, because no other good solution could be found.

When a penal institution such as this one, is looked at in an unbiased way, one sees the inmates on one side and the public servants on the other. The public servants' task is to carry out the inmate's sentences, the contents and goals of which are prescribed by law. Contact with the social workers is part of this sentence.

This constellation was a perfect example of the inner conflict that the social workers experienced as employees of the correctional facility they serve. They felt more solidarity with the prisoners than with the administration. The social workers are sometimes blind to the reality that they can go home in the evenings whereas the offenders whom they serve remain locked up. The inmates, on the other hand, are more aware of this reality and often have a hard time taking the social workers' idealistic commitment seriously. Instead, they often try to use the social workers to their own advantage.

Taking advantage of the social workers in this way is a provocation, because the social workers, too, have their limits as to how far they will allow themselves to be used.

When they say no, the limits are then established and the reality is put into the spotlight. This inner and outer conflict of becoming close to the inmates while establishing limits makes social work so difficult that many workers get "burned out" within just a few years.

What is the benefit of such a constellation, when a good resolution is not found? It shows the background of structural conflicts and their effects. Bringing to light the unknown entanglement(s) is important. The ability of the various groups to work together, within their limits, is a necessary prerequisite for rehabilitation to have a chance at success.

Men and Women

The topic, "Men and Women," in regards to family constellations is inexhaustible. What dynamics take place between men and women? What is the foundation of the orders that are encountered in constellations? Many possible variations appear, and at the same time, many themes repeat themselves.

From my perspective, family constellations are a way of discovering the depth of reality. Underneath our every day reality, deeper levels of reality lie hidden—realities of which we are often unaware. Family constellations lead us to this level and show a truth which, when encountered, can be enlightening.

The following constellation took place in the last hour of a one-week training course. A participant reported that in the past few days she had become conscious of having a fundamental fear of men. Due to the short time we had, I led a brief, symbolic constellation for her.

The participant first set up herself and then placed her "fear" directly behind herself. Across from the representative for herself, she set up a representative for "men," and across from him, a representative for "women."

The first thing was for the woman to turn around and face her fear. I proposed that she bow to her fear and express her respect for it. She did so, but then determined that it was not done in good faith. It did not correspond to her true feelings. She was relieved when she said to her fear, "I do not honor you. I want to get rid of you." She then looked at the representative for women and felt very connected to her. When she stood in front of the representative for women, she felt good and strong. The representative for women then said to her, "Fear is a part of life. I sometimes have fear and that includes having fear of men." The representatives for women and men then looked directly at each other. To the question, "How do you feel?" the representative for women said, "Fascinated. And I feel somewhat afraid." Therefore, I had her say this sentence directly to the men, "I am fascinated by you and somewhat afraid." I then proposed the same sentence, "I am fascinated by you and somewhat afraid," to the representative for the men. He said the sentence and also agreed with it.

Men and women are fundamentally different and because of this, will always be somewhat foreign to one another. These differences create fascination, but they also create fear. Fear can easily turn to aggression as a means of protection or defense. "Offense is the best defense," goes the expression. Coupled with those differences and fear, come the bad experiences that men and women have had with each other and feelings that are passed from generation to generation. In this way, age-old experiences set the tone of our lives as a man or a woman.

> A Swiss woman, about 60 years old, set up her family. She reported no special or traumatic events in her family history. She then mentioned somewhat off-handedly that her mother, at the request of her father and his family, had all of her teeth removed before the wedding, because this would help them save money in the future. I was shocked and I decided to have the mother's husband say, "I wanted you to have all of your teeth pulled and I take on the responsibility for that." However, he couldn't say it. I then set up the father-in-law. He said, "Women's teeth must be removed. There are many men who have come before me and we all have the opinion that women's teeth must be removed. Otherwise, they are too dangerous. "His own wife remained astonishingly peaceful and I proposed the sentence, which felt accurate to her, "I could be dangerous, but I don't want to be."
>
> In the discussion after the constellation, it came to light that removing the teeth of the bride was a common practice in some regions of Switzerland until about 40 years ago. Even the woman who set up the constellation had had eight of her teeth pulled, two on each side, top and bottom, when she was 18 years old, at her parents' request.

In a relationship, it is often the case, that if one of the partners is aggressive, the other is peaceful and patient. However, sometimes the dynamic found at a deeper level, is that the one who seems to all outward appearances to be the more peaceful person is really the more aggressive partner and the more aggressive one is actually more frightened, losing his temper as a means of defense. There is possibly a

healthy mechanism at work here, which allows only one partner to be aggressive. After all, what is the alternative? A
family constellation showed me what happens when aggression escalates in both partners.

> A woman sets up her family. The father had
> injured the mother badly during a fight. In the family
> constellation, both of them stand across from each
> other, full of hatred. Both of them want to be the
> strongest. It is shown that the woman knowingly pro-
> voked the man.
> The solution comes only as the daughter leaves
> the parents' responsibility to them and releases them
> from her heart. Both of the parents turn their backs
> to the family. Then a release of tension occurs for all
> of them.

When fights between a man and a woman escalate to
the point of physical violence, it begs the question: "Who will
kill whom and how?" The film "War of the Roses" was a bril-
liant satire about this battle between husband and wife. Both
sexes are capable of murderous aggression. It belongs to our
collective inheritance as human beings, as well as to our individual capabilities. We can see the aggressive potential of
men today, in wars and conflicts around the globe, be it in
Africa, Israel or Yugoslavia. It happens so often, that we get
used to it. Men kill other men and often, women and children
as well. The mass rapes, such as those that are reported to
have occurred in Yugoslavia, seem to be the unloading of
stark hatred.

The fact that women can hate in the same murderous
way as men, can carry as much anger in them as men can and
can similarly act out this anger, first became clear to me

through family constellations. A tremendous rage towards men resides in many women. They are often completely unaware of it. On the surface, it is visible as a lack of respect for men and a condescending attitude towards them. At the beginning of a seminar, during the first few constellations, this rage resides below the surface. Only after the first day or sometimes longer, does this rage fully reveal itself.

> A participant in a constellation wants to have the reasons for her difficulty in relationships with men resolved. She feels as if she is "incompetent" in that area of her life and suspects that it may have something to do with her relationship with her father. She had seven different relationships that lasted from half a year to three years and she set up all of these men in her constellation. She also set up an eighth man, her current boyfriend.
> She was able to honor the first three men and say goodbye to them. As she tried to do the same with the other men, she noticed that she no longer could perceive the men in any personal way. Other men could just as well have been standing there. The fourth man was angry and wanted to leave. Suddenly, the atmosphere was full of tension. A sentence came to her, "If someone here is going to leave, then it will be me!" Whereas she previously felt like a victim of her inability to relate to men, her suppressed anger now showed itself, coming swiftly to the surface. I then proposed that she say to her current boyfriend, "You're next." She confirmed that this sentence felt accurate.

The anger that shows itself here is an old one, which was passed on through many generations. The causes for it can't be found in the woman's own life. Her mother had this anger, as did her mother before her. It comes from the time that women had very little choice in life and had to accept hardships, while suppressing their feelings. In addition, the pain and violence that were experienced in war have contributed to this anger—the pain of losing the men in their lives (sons, husbands, fathers, lovers) as well as the harm experienced at the hands of men during wartime. This is why angry women from previous generations show up constantly in family constellations. These are women who have suppressed so much pain, that they have become resentful and embittered. The presence of this bitterness is strong and palpable. Such a woman often releases her anger within her own family, though she is often unaware of it, having the impression that her actions are appropriate to her current situation. However, even small situations can bring out tremendous anger, as she believes that the other person is the one to blame.

Not all aggression in a relationship is oriented toward the destruction or humiliation of the other person. It often serves another purpose in relationships. This is illustrated in the case with a client whose family was set up by a therapist who wanted to inspect his own work.

> The client had been suffering from a disease for fifteen years. Along with the medication that is covered by her insurance, she received money from her husband for alternative medical treatment. A new, very expensive, alternative procedure had recently become available. Her husband had some money left over from an inheritance, but he wanted to use it to take a trip to China, rather than pay for additional treatment for his wife.
>
> In the constellation, she is standing at a distance, across from her husband, who has made a fist with one hand, resting it in the palm of the other. He says the sentence, "If I don't hold on to this arm, I will

kill you." He has a murderous anger towards his wife. The woman's reaction to his statement is at first neutral. The sentences that she finds accurate are, "I am above you and your anger. I do not honor you and I am angry, too. For fifteen years, I have only taken from you."

The solution is found when the man says to her, "That's enough." The woman smiles at him and says, "Finally." The man admits his part in the escalation of aggression, saying, "I haven't behaved in a way that is easy to respect." The woman states, "I provoke you because I want to respect you." Both of them are able to come closer and they smile at each other, as the man says once again, "But I'm still going to China!"

This constellation reveals a pattern often found in relationships. The woman provokes the man in order to see his anger. It is difficult for many men to show anger in an acceptable fashion and they suppress it. If a man never becomes angry, however, he withholds an essential part of his strength. Setting limits allows for mutual respect.

Perhaps ironically, women get angry if they never see their man get angry! The woman has an enormous need to see that anger—*not* as violence, but as power and strength. The risk for the woman is that the man is not able to control his anger. If the man is able to express his anger without becoming violent, it makes many women feel relieved. "Finally!" said the woman in the last constellation. She was pleased to see her husband no longer let people do whatever they want with him (including her!), but rather, in a controlled manner, draw a line. This would not be the dynamic or her feeling ("Finally!") if his anger turned into physical abuse.

To paraphrase Daniel Goleman, men tend to become "flooded" with strong feelings, such as anger, more easily than women. If a person becomes flooded with feelings, he can lose control, be unable to sort out his thoughts and resort to primitive reactions. Psychologically, this flooding can be recognized when a person's pulse rises ten, 20 or even 30 beats per minute within seconds.

In a relationship, men tend to be flooded with feelings faster (albeit starting at a lower intensity of anger) than women. Research shows that men's pulse usually accelerates to a higher speed quicker than that of their wives. However, their pulse also immediately slows down by ten beats per minute when they begin to calm down. It works like a healthy protection mechanism, ensuring that the anger does not get out of control. This helps both people, first the man and then the woman.

The dilemma, however, is this: At the same time that the man calms down, the woman's pulse speeds up tremendously. The woman is now more tense than the man, and the next victim of the phenomenon of "flooding".

Aggression among men and aggression between men and women often have different orientations and goals. (I have not personally encountered aggression between women in any of my constellations thus far, which is why I don't include it here.) Aggression between men is more "one-dimensional."

> A daughter sets up her family. Her father had trusted her with a secret. He had killed a man in Africa. She is the only one who knows about it and this secret is a heavy burden to carry. We set up both men as well as the daughter.
> The father is afraid of the other man. The other man is hostile, prepared to engage in a fight and feels superior. He states, "I am stronger than you." I propose this reply to the father, "But I killed you and I

was stronger." The father adds, "And I was quicker." The other man cannot accept the fact that he died. He still feels stronger. The tension remains.

The solution comes when I have both of them bow to each other. That finally brings a sense of relief as well as respect between them. (It is still important for the father to tell the daughter that he was wrong to tell her this, creating a secret between them.)

At times, aggression between men is more of a ritual contest of strength. Underneath the surface of such contests, there is actually a type of partnership. The conflict is perceived as more of a sport than something personal. The mutual bowing that takes place, similar to the bowing that takes place in Asian martial arts before the fight begins, expresses this partnership in the best possible way. Such a bow releases tensions in constellations as well.

In contests of strength in athletics, the end is also ritualized. In wrestling, the loser, pinned to the ground, taps on the floor three times and the match is over. However, when it is clear that the fight is about life or death, then death belongs to one of the possible results and is accepted without animosity. I have repeatedly experienced constellations in which soldiers on enemy sides faced each other and neither side blamed the other or held a grudge, despite the fact that one soldier had killed the other.

Would such a bow be logical or appropriate in a contest of strength between a man and a woman? My wife and I discussed this question after the previously mentioned constellation and we both came to the same conclusion. The answer is no.

What would be an appropriate ending? Tapping three times on the floor? Again, we came almost simultaneously to the following conclusion: The "appropriate" end to a "real" contest of strength where the man wins would be for them to sleep together—given that both of them agreed to the contest. To be perfectly clear and avoid misunderstandings, what is meant by this is *not* that the man forces the woman into a fight and then takes her to bed. Rape is *not* what is meant here, nor is it ever sanctioned! What is meant is rather a mutually satisfactory ending that celebrates the respect that comes from a fair fight between partners who admire each other's strengths.

On the other hand, when the woman is stronger, she rejects the man, and disrespects him. My wife remembers occasions when she had won a contest of strength, be it emotional or intellectual, against a man. She felt a short moment of triumph, which was followed by a slight disdain for the man. She no longer considered him to be a "real man."

These archaic images are reflected in the German tale of Brunhilde and Siegfried. The physically strong and almost unconquerable Brunhilde is conquered by the invisible Siegfried. King Gunther takes credit for "conquering" her and marries her. On their wedding night, though, Brunhilde hangs King Gunther from the window, showing that he is weaker than she. For him she feels only disdain. Then Brunhilde gives herself willingly to Siegfried, though he is stronger than she.

What purpose does such an archaic contest of strength between a man and a woman serve? It makes sense when attracting a mate. The man is only allowed to be the woman's partner if he is stronger than her. In that way, he shows the woman that he is capable of protecting her. Only then can the woman give herself fully to him.

Respect is the outcome of the contest of strength. The man is no different than the woman in this way. He, too, likes the challenge. If the woman makes it too easy for him, it is

then difficult for him to earn respect, in which case there
will be no bond between them. A man wants a woman who
challenges him. He can then respect her, which is how the
bond succeeds.

This is why the concept of "conquering" or "being conquered" does not pertain to a contest of strength between a
man and a woman. If it leads to a bond, there is no winner or
loser. In sex, too, there is no winner or loser. After all, who
would be the winner and who would be the loser? The man
or the woman? Winning and losing is inappropriate in this
context.

What happens after one attracts a mate and a bond is
established? Bert Hellinger describes it in this way: "The
woman follows the man, and the man serves the feminine."
What does he mean by this? What is behind this statement?

It is shown in family constellations that the person who
is responsible for security stands in the first place. Until now,
in our culture, the man was responsible for the security of the
family. The old image was that the man takes care of the
family's survival, which means it is his job to protect the wife
and children and to provide for them. One role, which he
must take on, is that of the warrior, in the sense that he must
defend against physical threats. This is why it is so important
that the man possess the necessary strength. This role is still
part of a man's identity, even if he is not aware of it in everyday life. A friend of mine who works with criminal offenders
told me about a couple who was robbed. The robber threatened them with a knife while they were in their car. The man
felt traumatized by the fact that he was not able to live up to
his role of protector.

Survivors of the World War II concentration camps in
Germany have similar stories. The most painful degradation

for the Jewish men was that they were powerless and humiliated in front of their wives and children and could not fulfill their role as protector.

Aside from defending the family against threats, the man earns an income. He is responsible for creating the most secure "nest" possible. He represents the family in the outside world and connects them to it. He leads the family into the outside world and that is why the woman follows him.

During pregnancy as well as during the first few years of the child's life, the woman is in need of support. The man "builds the nest," so that the children have a safe place in which to grow up. The woman brings the children into the world, gives them milk and cares for them. That is the feminine which the man serves.

In the order between the man and the woman, the direction they are facing together, is always toward the third place—the children. The man and the woman serve this third place in the best possible manner. The ranking corresponds to each person's function and is not a judgment of worth.

This is made clear by examples from two different constellations:

> A grandmother died while giving birth. The grandchildren are afraid to have children themselves. The grandmother's death was a traumatic event in the family with far-reaching consequences that spread across many generations. The grandfather felt guilty for her death because he was the one who impregnated her.
>
> His wife stands across from him in the constellation and says to him: "To die while giving birth is a risk I carry by being a woman and I accept the risk and live with it. You are only my husband." The man is then able to relax and his feelings of guilt dissolve.

Women risk their lives when they give birth. Before the developments of modern medicine, more than one-third of women died in childbirth. Is there any such comparable risk for men? Here's an example:

> The client's father was part of the resistance movement in Belgium during the war and he died in a concentration camp. In the constellation, his wife—the client's mother—was full of guilt because she did not fight alongside him.
>
> The following sentences for the man brought a solution, "You are a woman and I am a man. Women take on the risks of childbirth and men take on the risks of war." The woman relaxed and was able to release her guilt.

Originally, each gender had tasks to perform which bore related risks. Family constellations reflect those archaic principles, over and over again. In spite of all of the change we have experienced in our society, these old roles still live on inside of us. This remains valid regardless of whether a person denies it or ignores it. The old role is there, hidden and undiscovered. When a person recognizes and respects this order, however, he becomes more aware and that awareness results in greater freedom.

The first position in a family constellation conveys this meaning. As previously mentioned, the person who stands in the first position is responsible for the family's security. At the beginning of many constellations, the woman stands in the first position and the man in the second position. Occasionally this is the order where both partners and the children feel best. Often, though, it is a relief for the wife and children when the man takes the first place. He feels stronger and more responsible for the family. The wife and children relax and feel more secure.

In today's society, the orders that bring resolution in many family constellations seem to have become outdated and superfluous. The average number of children per household in the western world continues to drop. People no longer raise ten or fifteen children, but rather only one or two. With the advent of the birth control pill, practically every woman has access to reliable birth control for the first time in history. The enormous amount of energy needed by parents to raise a dozen children is now freed up. In theory, the man, being the breadwinner, has more energy and the woman as the birth- and caregiver, has more as well.

So many possibilities and alternatives are developed in our culture that it often seems as if culture can be shaped any way one would like. Below the surface, though, the old programs for survival remain. They are often the reason why an inexplicable dissatisfaction occurs in some situations. If the situation requires it, then the old survival programs are immediately re-activated.

When a woman becomes pregnant, sometimes these old principles show up in a way that even surprises the woman herself. A lot of mindsets that used to seem clear and distinct suddenly become less so during the vulnerable state of pregnancy. A side of the woman that she herself didn't even know existed might show itself. The child, too, once born, has the power to topple the most well planned out life and career paths of both parents.

Just watching the evening news can show us just how quickly circumstances bring us from frivolity to gravity. Wars, between and within countries, are being waged in many parts of the world. We are surrounded by them and within a week, a month or even a moment, our country can be pulled into it. That's how it was in the first half of the twentieth century when millions of men were sent off to fight the First and Second World Wars.

In addition, modern technology has made our previous "programming" for survival practically meaningless, for in most parts of the world (though not all parts!), the old ideas of how the man must go away and fight for his family, village or country, have been replaced by new ideas. The "old" orders are no longer the accepted reality. Technology has made the world "smaller". There is no "over there." Every war is much closer than before and civilians are caught in the merciless battles (though the Thirty Years War in the 1600's may have been no different.) Buying or developing a better weapon used to be part of a man's duty to defend his family, but even this has become absurd in today's world. The proliferation of newer, more lethal weapons only serves to heighten the danger for all and cause more insecurity.

Today, we find ourselves in a conflict between the old orders and the new. The old orders still function to some small degree, while the new orders have not yet been firmly established. Family constellations can help us recognize which of the old orders still exist within us.

The Concept of "Homeland" as Shown in the German Inheritance of the Third Reich

One part of human bonding has to do with nationality—the country that a person comes from. There are many questions regarding nationality, such as: Are there ways in which we are all alike? Are Germans like other groups of people? How are they different?

When Germans search for their family's roots in family constellations, they eventually run into a certain word. That word is "homeland." What does the word "homeland" mean to a German? Is it perhaps just a romantic, yet outdated concept? And what of the images of dying for one's country, of right-wing ideology and outdated conservative values that the word also evokes? Many Germans nowadays dream about emigrating and living in other countries. The new ideal is that of the cosmopolitan, a wanderer who feels at home in cities and countries all over the world. The concept of "homeland" seems to be losing its meaning.

A small episode in Buenos Aires shows how strong a person's connection to their homeland is. A 60-year-old Argentinean woman, whose German parents immigrated to Argentina before she was born, told me the following story. She was watching Germany compete against Argentina in the soccer World Cup. When Germany scored the first goal, she spontaneously broke into cheers, only to be faced with expressions of alienation from her friends.

Family constellations give us a new understanding of what "homeland" means. The topic of "homeland" often comes to the foreground in family constellations when a person's homeland is lost or the person is forced to leave it. In cases of expulsion and emigration, as well as when the client has parents of different nationalities, a representative for each country can be set up. A person could represent, for example, East Prussia or Yugoslavia or Brazil. Like representatives for family members, the representative for a country also perceives feelings. The person who represents a country usually feels a sense of peace and strength.

The person whose homeland is set up feels a strong relationship to the homeland. Setting up the homeland often gives the client a sense of peace and relief, as it does, for example, in the family constellations of Germans who were forced to flee from East Prussia and Silesia after the Second World War. The strong bond to a person's homeland becomes visible. This bond is not broken even when the client leaves their country.

The effect of this loss is similar to losing a beloved family member. If the loss is suppressed, there remains an emotional wound which weakens a person. The wound is only healed when a place is made for the pain. Resolution comes when the homeland is given its place in the constellation, a place where it is honored and in which it belongs.

Another client states that he often feels powerless and weak. His father had to leave East Prussia, where the family had resided for many generations.

> A participant is set up in the background to represent East Prussia. The father is drawn to the homeland. He turns around and feels great pain over the loss. The strength comes back when he bows and says to the homeland, "You are my homeland and you have a big place in my heart." The son prefers to look away from East Prussia, though at the suggestion from the therapist, he faces it and looks at it. He bows and says, "I honor you as the homeland of my father and I give you a place in my heart." He now feels relaxed and more peaceful.

Some children disregard or reject their parents' homeland, devoting themselves completely to their new home. When they do this, however, they lose an important part of their strength as well as losing their roots. One sentence which has a good effect in these situations in family constellations is, "I honor you as the homeland of my parents and I give you a place in my heart." In this way, the child honors his own roots and becomes stronger.

A constellation, which Bert Hellinger carried out with German Jews in February 1998, in Frankfurt, Germany, helps deepen our understanding of this concept of "homeland." At the beginning of the Third Reich, the parents fled to (what was still known as) Palestine, where their son was born and lived until he was 11. Thereafter, he lived in Germany and considers himself a German.

> In his constellation, representatives were chosen for Germany and for Israel. Israel felt as if it wasn't being seen or honored. An important step towards a solution for both the parents and the son was when Israel came to the foreground and was honored.
>
> However, the Jewish son did not feel good at his parents' side. Something seemed to be missing. He still felt like he was without a homeland. Acting on intuition, Hellinger chose a family to represent the Palestinians who had been driven from Israel and set them up across from Israel. The client felt as if he were being pulled to the refugees' side. When he stood next to them, he was able to relax. Here—at the side of the Palestinian refugees—is where he felt he belonged.

Expulsion is always an injustice towards those expelled. The newcomers who take the land into their possession profit from this injustice. The desire to compensate and to atone arises in the children and grandchildren of the aggressors. In this constellation, the need to compensate was shown by the fact that the Jewish son could not accept Israel as his home, but rather took on the victims' feelings of homelessness. (Similar effects resulted from the Native American genocide in the United States, and will be discussed below.)

What connects Germans to their past and especially with the Third Reich? The tenth World Congress on Family Therapy in 1998, in Düsseldorf, Germany, was opened by Israel Charney, the former president of the World Therapy Organization. He began his speech with the statement, "I will never forgive the Holocaust." Shock waves ran though the audience. The Third Reich and the Holocaust were thrust from the distant past into the present.

Family constellations among Germans show how World War II and the Third Reich still reside in the German psyche. Our inheritance of this history is different than that of other nations. Repeatedly in constellations, we encounter guilt and injustice, perpetrators and victims, as well as many brothers, sons and fathers who died in the war. Generations of children and grandchildren are connected to them.

A constellation led by a colleague and myself a few years ago greatly broadened my horizons. Until this time, I found the media's constant preoccupation with the Third Reich exaggerated and burdensome. I was of the opinion that one shouldn't be preoccupied with it and should look instead to the future. I am not personally burdened by a family history of Nazism, because my parents had developed an aversion to the ideology due to their Catholic beliefs. My father was a doctor in the war and had barely survived.

> A 40-year-old man, who came across like much younger man, had difficulty with relationships. He set up his family and it came to light that his grandfather was an enthusiastic Nazi.

The grandfather stood in the room with a powerful presence. He seemed to be idealistic and excited about the Nazi ideology. The man himself was fascinated by his grandfather—by his strength and by his ideals. In order to bring the criminal reality of what happened into the foreground, we added some representatives of Nazi perpetrators and victims to the group. Without distinguishing between them, two of the new people set up felt like they were victims and two felt like perpetrators. The grandfather and the grandchild were resistant to looking at them and only able to do so with a great deal of effort. The ideals and ideas of the Nazis seemed to continue to blind them to reality.

In this constellation, one could sense the original fascination with Nazi ideology. The attraction to this way of thinking worked through the grandfather down the generations to his grandchild. The man had not completely resolved this issue during the constellation. A year later, in a similar constellation, he was able to look at the feelings he had taken on and gain some inner distance to them.

After this constellation, I suddenly got the feeling that I, too, am in the same boat as he is and have to face this past. I am no longer so surprised by the huge amount of press there is, even now, about the Third Reich. Collectively, we are still so tied to it that it comes up as a topic over and over again. It seems to me, that through the merciless annhilation of the Jews and other groups during the decade before 1945, an entire population succeeded in burdening itself with guilt. Some more than others, but almost everyone, due to his actions or inactions, in some way collaborated in it. Therefore, almost everyone carried a piece of that guilt.

As Bayohr proved in a newly publicized doctoral thesis, the total property of at least 30,000 households of murdered or expelled Jews was auctioned in Hamburg alone. He calculated a total of 10,000 buyers and estimated that there must be millions of similar buyers nationwide. That means that millions of Germans have profited directly from the killing of the Jews.

It appears to me, then, that the children and grandchildren of this generation have three alternatives:

If the children have taken on the parents' guilt and shame, the first alternative is for them to accept their parents, along with the guilt that emerged after Germany's defeat in World War II and the collapse of the Third Reich. They feel as guilty as their parents and carry this guilt down through the generations. In this example, it is embarrassing for a German who goes to a foreign country. He is relieved when someone thinks that he is French or American. This is most noticeable when a German meets a Jewish person. One feels a certain self-consciousness and insecurity.

The second alternative is that the children reject their guilt-ridden parents and blame them. The children in this case, without roots, will be weak. If a child denies his parents and judges them, he cuts off the power that flows to him from the previous generations, through the parents.

The third possibility? The third possibility is for the children to put on combat boots, shave their heads and beat up foreigners and other "unacceptable" segments of the population. When they do that, they are accepting their fathers as they were before the collapse of the Third Reich. They are then like the parents in the way of their actions and guilt, but they also have the parents' strength.

Robert Leicht proposed a solution for this a dilemma in an editorial in the German newspaper *die Zeit*:

Is it possible that Germany's history and present continue to operate under the principle of responsibility for the deeds of the Third Reich even after all of the people who experienced the Holocaust, all of the perpetrators and victims—even all of their children—are no longer alive? A comparison with inheritance law may give us a clue. A person may receive an inheritance only in its entirety, with debit and credit. If a person refuses the debt (or the guilt), then the inheritance must be disclaimed. If a person rejects an inheritance, however, he is acting irresponsibly. Such a person wants to remain faceless. Such a person hopes to avoid responsibility.

Does this mean the grandchildren also inherit the debts (or guilt) of their grandparents, to the point that a young German adult, born in 1970, feels shame when he meets a Jew of the same age?

Leicht confused things somewhat with the use of the terms "debt" and "guilt." This is differentiated in inheritance law. If a person gains from the inheritance (i.e., if there is more capital inherited than debt), then the inheritor must also pay off the debts. This does not mean, however, that the inheritor takes on the deceased one's guilt. This is personal and belongs to the deceased. A son, for example, does not go to prison for a deceased father who committed an offense. However, when the father dies, the son does take care of the debts that the father had taken upon himself.

This means that it is our job as Germans to take responsibility for the damages caused by our parents. Otherwise, we would continue to profit from the injustices of the Third Reich. For example, a grandfather had made a "great buy" during the Third Reich. He purchased a company owned by his Jewish neighbor for a fraction of the company's actual value. The grandchild, being the heir to the company, remains bonded to the injustice committed by his grandfather. A family constellation led by Bert Hellinger and related in the book *Der Abschied*, shows how much of an effect such an injustice has.

> The woman's father had been a Nazi and had taken over a Jewish business in Prague during the war. The woman suffered from severe bouts of Angst. Her brother was schizophrenic and had committed suicide. In the constellation, Hellinger added the Jewish businessman to the constellation.
>
> *The Jewish businessman:* "I can only focus on one place. I keep thinking, 'Oh God, oh God, oh God.' I feel hot, and I can only look at one place. I feel like I'm in a panic and am rooted to one spot. When the woman's father speaks, I feel somewhat relieved."
>
> *Hellinger to the woman's father:* "I will place you here in front of him."
>
> *Hellinger to the Jewish businessman:* "How do you feel now?"
>
> *Jewish businessman:* "I am simply afraid. I feel like I am being pulled backwards and my voice is failing me. I feel threatened."
>
> *Hellinger to the woman's father:* "And you?"
>
> *Father:* "I am fairly calm, without any particular positive or negative feelings."
>
> *Hellinger to the Jewish businessman:* "What is going on with you?"
>
> *Jewish businessman:* "He has a very strong, stoic power. He looks much larger than he is."
>
> The constellation reaches a satisfactory conclusion only after the father follows the Jewish businessman, who is presumed dead.

What do constellations achieve? There is a bond on a new level without taking on the guilt. Constellations make possible the healing step to this new level. The child honors the mother or the father as the giver of his life and he leaves the responsibility for their actions with them. This way, the child can remain connected to his roots without taking on guilt, which does not belong to him.

> A participant in a seminar asked Bert Hellinger, "I understand that it is very important for a person to go back to their roots. But what is a person to do when they are ashamed of their roots and of their ancestors? My grandparents were Nazis and I feel ashamed when I think of them. So I avoid looking at my roots."
>
> Hellinger answered, "When a person is ashamed like this, it means he is trying to escape a fate that he shares with others. But it doesn't work. That feeling of shame originates from an attitude of superiority. That kind of attitude, though, would be no better than the attitude the Nazis had towards Jews and other peoples. This attitude connects a person to the perpetrators instead of to the victims. Sadness and honor connects us to the victims. These feelings are the opposite of shame and they are the appropriate feelings toward the victims. We cannot simply elevate ourselves above a perpetrator and believe that we are better. At some deeper level, we need to recognize that we are connected to them and that when we die, there will no longer be any difference between them and us."

The image that I have of the situation between Jews and Germans is this: Say, for example, that there was a brutal murder in a family. One brother killed another brother and almost killed the whole family. One day, the murderer's children encounter the children of the victim. How are they supposed to get along with one another? What are their common roots? In family constellations, we encounter what happened in the Third Reich at a very personal level. There are people—the children and grandchildren of the perpetrators and victims—who are effected by what went on at that time. Family constellations, though, are about taking ownership of pain and guilt.

At the same time, the Third Reich has a certain collective side and it is enormous. It seems to me that National Socialism and its ideas came along like a huge collective wave, which appeared unexpectedly and was of such size and intensity that many individuals got swept along in it. It was similar to the way that a tsunami, caused by unseen underwater earthquakes, races across the surface of the ocean with an enormous destructive potential, under a clear, blue sky.

The truth is, we do not really understand the cause of it. We cannot understand it. It is beyond our capacity. The wave is past, however, and it seems as though we are now standing on firmer ground. But beneath it all, the shocking possibility remains: What would happen if another such wave were to come? We try to fight our feelings of helplessness with analysis and attempts to "individualize" it. The fact is, though, that we are helpless, standing there in the face of the terror that happened at that time.

At times, I have even set up a representative for life itself in a constellation. The only suitable way of facing life was with a deep, respectful bow. Life is bigger than we are. This occurrence—the Third Reich—is bigger than us, and it is a part of life.

National Similarities and Differences

This work with family constellations has been developed in the last 20 years in areas where German is spoken (Germany, Austria and Switzerland). A question, which soon arose, was: has Bert Hellinger discovered orders which are typically German or are they applicable in other countries as well? This question has since been answered by therapists who have brought family constellations to other parts of the world. I myself have gained experience with constellations in other countries—Switzerland, Spain, Italy, Argentina, USA, Australia, New Zealand, Russia and India—and have carried out constellations with groups of Japanese and Taiwanese people. In the past several years, after developing the foundations of the work in Germany, Bert Hellinger himself is going out into the world to bring this type of therapy to other countries.

What similarities and differences are to be found from country to country? I can only relate my personal experiences rather than giving statistical evidence. However, the experiences are informative, because they show families and nations from a new perspective.

A great similarity exists among the countries that engaged in war within the last two generations. The result of war is the deaths of many young soldiers. Parents lose their children, sisters lose their brothers, wives lose their husbands and children are born who will never know their fathers, because they died before the birth.

In German constellations, it has been seen how painful the loss of a brother was for a sister. The surviving sister is often preoccupied with an inclination to die. Their children sense it, take it on and themselves develop this inclination to die. However, the same pain occurs in other nations as well.

Death can have various effects. There are deaths that are experienced collectively and especially traumatically. Consequently, the memory of these deaths is repressed from consciousness as much as possible and weighs heavily, deep within the family soul. In a constellation, the representatives give a slight shudder when these deaths are mentioned. In Germany, these are the deaths that occurred in concentration camps. In Japan, they are the deaths that occurred when the atomic bombs were dropped on Hiroshima and Nagasaki. In the United States, these are the deaths of the Native Americans.

A loss is especially enduring when the family is unsure of the death. That is the case, for example, of the fate of the men in Argentina who disappeared—kidnapped under the dictatorship—the so-called desaparecidos. Even today, many years later, the families of the deceased gather regularly in Buenos Aires to demonstrate.

A Constellation in Germany showed me how difficult it is to deal with those who are missing.

> The client suffers from severe feelings of guilt. His father had a brother who was missing in action in World War II. At the end of the 1950's, the father had his brother—who at that time had been missing for over fifteen years—declared dead so that the inheritance could finally be settled.
>
> In the constellation, it is shown that the father secretly felt an enormous amount of guilt, almost as if he, through the act of applying for a death certificate for his brother, was his brother's murderer.

When I observe other European nations, their connectedness and family ties seem stronger than in Germany. Their roots seem to be more intact. The only country whose population seems to have even fewer roots, is the United States. That is evident in Americans' constant changes in career, private life and address.

The American writer Norman Mailer opined on the topic that this phenomenon shows itself in a unique manner: personal uprooting. Few Americans today could find the house that they were born in. That is why Mailer believes that Americans are more fearful than people in other countries, even if that can't be proven. He suspects that the average American has more fear than the average Frenchman, German or Englishman, although these countries also have severe historical influences and certainly more overall suffering than the USA. What can explain this?

Perhaps it is because the land was taken by people who were uprooted themselves—immigrants—destroying and driving away the people whose land it was—the Native Americans. Additionally, thousands of Africans and other Third World peoples were used as slaves in order to work the land and obtain wealth. I suspect that a mechanism similar to that in Germany is at work: The ancestors' guilt burdens their children and further descendants.

The following family constellation, which Bert Hellinger led in 1998, in the USA, showed the unexpected dimensions of the bonds to the actions of one's ancestors. The client was a 44-year-old American who felt powerless—unable to find peace, feeling nowhere at home. His father had committed suicide fifteen years before.

In the constellation, the client and his five siblings feel isolated and unconnected. Through questioning, Hellinger finds out that the client's great-grandfather

built a railroad from Toronto to Boston in the middle
of the 19th century and had made a lot of money in
the venture.

The client talks about a recurring nightmare he
has, though. In the dream, he is riding in the car of a
train, up a mountainside to the peak. Suddenly there are
no more train tracks and the car plummets down the
side of the mountain. Hellinger sets up four men who
represent men who died during the construction of the
railroad. One of them sinks to the floor, feeling weak
and powerless. The client feels very connected to this
man and he cries, holds him and then bows, on his
knees, to him. The victim feels honored and he forgives.

This constellation shows what happens when a person
gets rich in a way that transgressed upon others. The guilt is
taken on by the children, grandchildren and great-grandchildren, who attempt to atone for it. When one looks at the
wealth that has accumulated in the USA by taking advantage
of others or the riches obtained by European countries in the
exploitation of other nations, the burden taken on by the
future generations is almost immeasurable! We can conclude
that the consequences of that which we call "imperialism" and
"capitalism" could perhaps explain a lot of the world's current
chaos and violence, which seem otherwise inexplicable.

When we look at the existing military conflicts around
the world today and the countless deaths that are attributed
to them, we must face the tragedy that is occurring and antic-
ipate the consequences for future generations.

My colleague, Sneh Victoria Schnabel, was invited to the
USA to conduct the first family constellations with Native
Americans. She described to me how extensive the tragedy
was and the ongoing devastation of the surviving Native
Americans over the last five or six generations. The atmos-

phere was comparable to the atmosphere during family constellations in which the theme is the Holocaust. The constellations were punctuated with shock and deep pain. Strength came into the families only after the generations, which lived before the fatal encounters with whites, were set up. After the two-day seminar, a Native American participant came to Sneh and told her of his countless attempts at Western types of therapy. He found that these therapies were unsuited to Native American problems. After this workshop, he finally felt that he had found something suitable and fruitful for the issues faced by Native Americans.

Are their islands in this sea of entanglements? What about constellations in countries that have been spared from war and campaigns of destruction? I would like to illustrate with my impressions from a six-day seminar with a group of Swiss people.

The first two days went rather leisurely. This is different from the German seminars, where the deaths from World War II come up immediately—the fathers, brothers and children who died in the war. It appeared that lucky circumstances protected the Swiss from such tragedies. The intensity of the seminar was fairly low.

On the third day, however, the issues, which these civil, middle-class families had suppressed, broke forcefully through to the surface. There was a constellation in which a pastor committed adultery with the woman who was to become his son's mother-in-law. The woman bore the pastor's child, but then claimed it was her husband's child. In other constellations, abuse came to the surface. Many families secretly had at least one "black sheep" who took on and carried the negative burden of the family. Those who took part in the seminars controlled their emotions to a high degree, requiring much energy to do so. When they could no longer maintain this control, suppressed feelings came out dramatically and uncontrollably.

Family constellations among non-western cultures are especially interesting as well. For instance, how are family constellations among Japanese or Taiwanese people different than they are in the West? The constellations were, for the most part, very similar to each other, more so than German constellations. The representatives of father and mother stood far apart and turned their backs on one another. When they turned around and looked at each other, they felt foreign to one another. None of them seemed to be together out of love. Many marriages had been arranged. The result was mutual disappointment and frustration, from which, in the best-case scenario, came a sense of comradeship in the midst of a difficult situation. A statement, which brought relief for one such couple, was, "You frustrate me and I frustrate you. We're in the same boat."

The women were especially unwilling to take on responsibility for marrying their partners. They saw themselves as victims. The strength to be responsible came only when the mother was placed behind the daughter and the daughter leaned against her. This was different than in German constellations.

At the same time, there were surrogate lovers for the frustrated parents. Almost always, erotic tendencies between the mother and a favorite son and between the father and a favorite daughter were visible. In German constellations, it is often the case that a child takes over the role of a parent, which increases the danger of the child being abused. Erotic feelings between a parent and child, however, most often result from a child representing an earlier lover or fiancé of the parent.

A Japanese daughter sets up her family. After the conflicts have been cleared up, the parents stand beside each other, across from the children. It seems as though the order is almost right. However, there is clearly an erotic tension between the father and the youngest daughter. The following sentences often help in such situations, for instance, "I am only your father and no more." Or, "I am only your daughter and no more," brought no change.

I was certain that the father had a first love, but the client told me that it was the first relationship for both parents. I finally risked an experiment and set up a woman to represent this first love. The father bent over as he saw the woman and then he beamed at her. He thought for a moment, and then gave his conclusion, "It is my mother."

The strong erotic connection these children have to their parents hinders their having fulfilling relationships of their own later on in life. Instead, they, too, turn to a child for this fulfilling relationship. This pattern is relived from one generation to the next. Even the other children, out of loyalty to the parents' mistakes and misfortunes, rarely have a fulfilling love relationship.

I was fascinated by a constellation with a Taiwanese woman whose sister died an early death. The deceased sister still belonged to the family in every way. Even a place at the table was always set for her. In the constellation, at first, the deceased sister was seen as dangerous and threatening. The surviving sister was afraid of her, much more so than in similar situations in German constellations. When the deceased sister said, "I died and you lived," a measure of peace was found.

People who are familiar with the strong effect that an early death has in German family constellations might suspect that things are different in cultures, which have rituals for honoring the dead. Constellations in those cultures, though, show the opposite. It appears that even in cultures, which honor their dead, there is still an inclination towards death among the siblings of a deceased child. One sibling dies and another lives. This feeling of guilt that the survivors have is not relieved by a cultural ritual for the dead. Not only that, idealizing the dead is a way of pushing her away, resisting the feelings that are surely there.

Family constellations are new to our culture, but the knowledge of a "Knowing Field" exists in other cultures. Here is an example from Mozambique: The psychologist Boia Efraime Junior, who studied at a German university, has worked tirelessly for years, in efforts to free abused children (mostly child soldiers) of their nightmares. He reported of his experiences with Mauro, who, at the age of twelve, was forced to watch helplessly as his father was killed. In the years thereafter, he was forced to kill as a child soldier. Nothing seemed to help him and with the permission of Efraime, a neighbor brought him to a *curandera*—a traditional healer. She celebrated a *Kufemba*-ritual:

> While in a trance, she contacted the souls of the victims and the relatives of the person who sought healing. Mauro first talked with his father and re-experienced his death and the conflict he felt because he was not able to help him. The father freed him of his guilt, telling him the soldiers had guns and were stronger. He assigned Mauro the task of planting a deciduous tree where they once lived and to use this tree as an altar. He could speak with him there whenever he wanted. Then, the souls of the victims that Mauro had killed appeared. He asked them for forgiveness and explained that he had been forced to kill in order to survive.

This is how Mauro encountered his father and was able to come into contact with his inner image of him. Other deceased persons also appeared. The similarities this has to a family constellation are amazing.

What kind of possibilities do family constellations provide us with in our torn world, where every day there seems to be new ethnic conflicts breaking out? It seems that there is understanding only on the surface. Hostility, hatred, murder and death break out repeatedly.

Constellations make it possible to reach a new depth of understanding of national conflicts. When a political conflict is set up, history comes alive and can be felt by the others. A workshop was conducted by Scheucher/Szyszkowitz on the conflict in Bosnia, during which they led a constellation.

About fifty people from various career fields came to this two-hour workshop. Two historians and an expert on southeastern Europe from the University of Graz, Austria, prepared a historical background for the constellation. Due to the fact that the conflict in Yugoslavia was so complex, the conflict in Bosnia was the focus, along with the question: What is needed for peace?

> The following parties were set up in the constellation: Serbia, Croatia, Yugoslavia, the Bosnian Serbs, the Bosnian Croatians, the Bosnian Muslims, the "undeclared" (those who do not identify themselves with any particular group), and the Austrian observers.
>
> The representative of the Bosnian Serbs felt as if he had been abandoned, as if he had no support behind him. Serbia stood in front of him in a confrontational way and was not prepared to give him any support. As an experiment, a representative for "Peace" was set up in the middle. The only party that

got any sense of relief from the representative for Peace was Bosnia. The representative for Peace felt so weak at this point, it seemed as if he might fall. For all of the other parties, Peace came too early, because their conflicts had not yet been worked out. The representative for Peace became progressively weaker and more pale, and seemed to draw attention away from the parties and their as of yet unspoken concerns and conflicts. The representative for Peace was then removed from the constellation.

An important step in the constellation came as the Austrians verbalized respect to Serbia. Then Serbia had a need to be honored and respected by Croatia. It was a very moving experience for the audience to observe how Croatia—with tears in his eyes—bowed deeply to Serbia and stated that he wanted to be recognized as a representative of Western culture. He stated that under this condition, he was prepared to honor Serbia as a representative of a great culture. The representative for the Austrians was then able to leave, satisfied. The representative for the "undeclared," who had previously been in a far corner of the room, was now ready to come closer to the others.

The old Yugoslavia was represented by a man in a wheelchair. He had to leave the constellation early, before it and the workshop ended. When he left the room, there was palpable relief felt by all. Everyone had the impression that the emerging understanding among the parties could be continued after the old multicultural and multinational Yugoslavian trauma honorably departed.

Family Constellations are a new and unique way to understand why some conflicts between nations or cultures continue and what is needed to find a good solution. It is not hard to imagine how politicians gain an inner image of what is needed for peace before they engage in peace talks.

Perhaps such a constellation could be videotaped and then shown on television, so that people in the relevant countries, as well as those fighting or entangled somehow with the conflicts, could witness it. I have noticed that the videos of Bert Hellinger conducting family constellations have a strong emotional effect on those watching. Why would a video of a political conflict be any different?

At this point, the findings of Anne Ancelin Schützenberger—the French researcher previously mentioned—would also be of value. She researches the meaning of historical occurrences (and repetitions) in our present lives. In parts of the Arabian world, the eight Christian crusades between 1096 and 1270 are still embedded in memory, as events that require atonement. For example, the Muslim, Ali Agca, justified his assassination attempt on Pope John Paul II thusly: "I have decided to kill Pope John Paul II, the supreme commander of the crusaders." (Mahr). We, too, carry the effects of such ancient historical events within us.

Constellations can help us achieve more understanding at the individual level, too, in fact, better than any other method I know of. A Japanese therapist, who has already taken the first steps towards family constellations with her countrymen, told me that the work has served as a type of "feeling school" for Japanese men. They fully repress their own feelings. However, as representatives, they find it easy to perceive and express feelings.

Representatives from one culture can experience what it feels like to belong to another culture, as well. In a constellation, which I carried out for Japanese participants, a German represented a Japanese wife. She described the first perceptions that she felt as a heat, which continued to rise within her. It took her a long time before she could cautiously formulate the sentence, "I believe my feeling is anger."

Later she told me that the way she perceived her feelings in that role was very different from the way that she perceived feelings while in the role of a German. For those who represent Germans, anger is usually immediately noticeable. In Japan, however, anger is something of a forbidden feeling, so that is how it is perceived by a European representative. Interestingly, a Japanese woman who represented a German woman noted to me how surprisingly strong and immediate was her perception of anger.

Likewise, in a constellation of an Indian family, I sensed that anger was a forbidden feeling—something like a taboo. On the other hand, an Indian who represented an Italian husband was able to perceive and articulate the feelings he felt with ease.

To represent people from another culture in a family constellation seems to be a way to gain a deeper understanding of life in a foreign culture. The more often a person takes on such roles, the more familiar he will become with the depths of the emotional structure of that culture.

Family Constellations and Ethics

We live in an age of superficiality. If something is possible, or doable, then it eventually it will be done—if not today, then tomorrow. The possibilities are endless. Thus, there was an article in *der Spiegel* entitled "There are No More Rules" with the following information: "US researchers have combined a human cell with the ovary of a cow and have isolated cells from the embryos which are incapable of dying. The researchers declared it to be a new era in medicine." There are ethics commissions, which rack their brains over such matters, without coming to any sort of meaningful, lasting.

The business of artificial insemination is booming. In the USA, it is possible to have five parents: the semen donor, the egg donor, a woman to bear the child and then the actual man and woman who raise the child.

Is there any end to it all? If so, where is the line drawn and who draws it? These questions are still open, and answers are needed. When these topics show up in family constellations, the constellations provide answers. They give reference to solutions that are suitable for the new questions.

Bert Hellinger, together with Hunter Beaumont, conducted family constellations on this topic in the USA (see *Wie Liebe Gelingt*). A client's second child, a daughter, came into being through artificial insemination with the semen of an unknown donor. All that was known about the donor was that he was Jewish. The marriage fell apart soon after the insemination. Here is a part of that constellation:

> *Husband:* "I feel very sad and isolated. I don't know who is who . . ."
> *Wife:* "I feel hostile towards my husband. I don't feel a connection with my daughter."
> *Daughter:* "I don't feel anything. I do feel, though, that I am being pulled backwards. When I heard that my father was Jewish, I felt a pain in my back . . ."
> *Hellinger:* You must refrain from having a father. You cannot have a father. Your mother cheated you out of him.
> (The mother's representative nods).
> *Hellinger (to the mother):* Look at her.
> (The mother faces the daughter).

Hellinger: Say to her: "I cheated you out of your father."

Wife: "I cheated you out of your father."

(Both of them look at one another for a long time).

Hellinger (to the daughter): How do you feel?

Daughter: "I am getting sad."

Hellinger: Tell her: "I will accept my life in this way, too."

Daughter: "'I accept my life in this way, too.' Yes, that feels right."

The mother and daughter look at each other and nod.

Hellinger (to the client): There is a way of ranking the family systems. The new system takes precedence over the old system. When a child comes from a new relationship, then the old relationship is over, which was the case here. When you and your wife decided on artificial insemination from the sperm of another man, your marriage was over. It was an unavoidable consequence of that decision.

Constellations bring us into contact with our inner authority, which cannot be influenced by arguments and justifications. The marriage fell apart. Nevertheless, it is important for the child to accept its life even at this price—even without a father.

Constellations shed light on other topics, too, in areas that we have taken for granted as a "normal" part of today's world. Here is part of a constellation regarding the case of a kidney transplant (from the book *Wo Demut heilt und Ohnmacht Frieden Stiftet*):

Rosemarie: Since I was three, I have had chronic kidney disease. By the time I was 21, both of my kidneys were completely dysfunctional. My father donated one of his kidneys to me at that time and it also became dysfunctional after four years. For the last six years, I have relied on kidney dialysis.

(The client sets up her father and herself. She is standing directly behind her father.)

The father starts to shake. After some time, he walks forward and lies down on his stomach. Rosemarie is swaying and seems as if she might fall. At the instruction of Bert Hellinger, she lies down on the floor next to her father and says,

Rosemarie: "What I demanded was too much . . ."

Father: "I feel as if dead is not dead enough. I want to go far away . . ."

(A short time later)

Father: "I gladly gave it to you, but it was too much."

After the constellation, *Hellinger says:* I would like to say something about organ transplants. The soul cannot handle it. Donating an organ does not serve love.

Client: That is how I felt about it! I was happy when it became dysfunctional!

The special thing about this constellation was that the father had donated one of his kidneys to his daughter. It is too much for the daughter to receive a kidney from her own father. Here is more of what Hellinger has said about organ transplants in general:

> In order for the transplant to go well, there must be a sense of community between the donor and the recipient—a deep love and respect. The recipient must have the blessing of the donor. Then it could work. But I wouldn't even do it from the start. I would neither donate an organ nor be the recipient of one. That is beyond what a human is capable of dealing with.

A good way to conclude this section on family constellations and ethics is with a quote from Hellinger:

> What I say is provocative and I do not claim to have the final say in things. That would not be my place to claim that. But what I say is worth taking into account.

EIGHT

What is Behind the Work with Family Constellations?

"Only the draft horse gets the whip."
Russian Proverb

Bert Hellinger's life's work and discoveries have touched a nerve in our modern times and interest in family constellations has grown in recent years, among experts and laymen alike. The attendance at family constellation seminars has increased immensely. It seems to be the only growth sector in the psychological market at the present time. Family constellations are booming.

But will family constellations have a lasting impact, or are they just one of those fads which resemble a wave—hitting the beach with huge, explosive power and then dissolving into mist. Aside from all of the excitement, questions arise about the concrete effects that the constellations produce, and about the long-term value of this work. There are also many critics of Family Constellations. Is there anything to this criticism?

Criticism and Objection

"Minds are divided on Hellinger," said a psychologist to me as we conversed on the topic of Family Constellations. It is difficult if not impossible to remain neutral about Bert Hellinger. He has the ability to polarize both laymen and experts. He has created many devotees on one side and bitter enemies on the other. There are many reasons for this division of minds. I will try to elaborate on some of those reasons and dissect them. It is astounding (or not) that most objections are directed at Bert Hellinger himself, instead of at family constellations themselves, which are usually not even addressed.

Bert Hellinger, born in 1925, has led a varied and full life. As a Christian missionary, life brought him to South Africa to work with the Zulus and 25 years later, in 1969, he left the priesthood and returned to Germany. He had already come into contact with group dynamics in South Africa, so decided to study psychology in Vienna. During that time, he went to the USA to study Primal Therapy with Art Janov. On his return, due to a presentation that he made on Primal Therapy, he was forced to leave the university before his student teaching began. He then focused on transactional analysis and during his work as a therapist he discovered that structures and "scripts" (life-defining patterns) regularly stem not from a person's own life, but from their family.

From this combination of script analysis, primal and family therapy, he developed his own way of setting up families. The thirst for knowledge has been a recurring theme throughout his life and he has been meticulous about judging only what comes from his own personal experience.

Today he devotes himself to his books and teaching videos, which here in Germany, have become best sellers simply through word of mouth. He now demonstrates his work, often with people who are seriously ill, in front of audiences, which range from 30 or 40 people to hundreds, even thousands at times. In addition he is spreading his work beyond the areas where German is spoken, teaching in many foreign countries.

Why are opinions about Hellinger so divided? The content of and the way in which he imparts his observations and knowledge is without compromise and rigorous and sometimes sounds quite harsh. One can be so absorbed in his direct approach, that he fails to notice the qualification or contradictory statement that he gives in the next sentence. Here is an example from an interview given by Hellinger to Norbert Linz.

> *Linz:* What are your most important therapeutic practices when giving a family constellation? How would you describe the main focus of that?
>
> *Hellinger:* I don't leave anything completely up to the client alone. For example, I don't let him seek the place where he feels the best on his own. I only allow it with the small things. When someone sets up their family, a picture of how the family's order is disrupted and how it can be brought into order emerges. That's what I follow when I seek a solution. So I am the one who changes these views of the family between the beginning and the end. And I set up the final view of the family as well. I arrange these views in cooperation with the client. Then I check these views according to the effect that they have— whether or not the effect confirms the view and whether or not further steps are necessary.

> *Linz:* So, you also test the inner picture the
> client has?
> *Hellinger:* I always have it tested no matter what.
> One doesn't need to believe what I say or do. But I
> don't leave the initiative up to the client. He wouldn't
> find the solution on his own. If he could do that, then
> he wouldn't need to come to me in the first place.
> When the resolving view of the family has been
> found, I let the client enter the picture himself and
> take over the place that his representative has been
> standing in. And so he himself tests whether or not
> the solution is the right one for him.

Such clear statements about the dominance of the therapist can at first be shocking—they are at least very unusual
on the therapy scene. In many psychotherapeutic arenas, it is
considered very important to leave the initiative to the client,
including him in the process as much as possible.

One can almost overlook the fact that Hellinger carefully
tests and checks the resolutions he proposes. And there's
more:

> *Linz:* But in your therapy groups, aren't some
> participants shocked at the direct way in which you
> confront them?
> *Hellinger:* I only confront the participant with a
> reality that is visible.
> *Linz:* Which *you* see!
> *Hellinger:* And which, of course, he knows him-
> self. That *is* shocking for people who don't want to see
> the truth.

Hellinger seems to be claiming that he knows all and
sees all! The inner critic in the reader may want to shout,
"Where does he get off feeling so sure of himself? Isn't that

just arrogance?" We are used to making everything relative to something else. It is almost foreign to us that a person would rely totally and completely on his perception and stand by it. We are generally skeptical of our own perceptions as well as those of others. In *Psychologie heute*, Ursula Nuber described it in this way: "So free of doubt, so sure of his judgments and unaffected by criticism and yes, such an authoritarian manner—no one has risked being this way for a very long time and absolutely not in a therapeutic context."

In addition, there is something about Hellinger which can either confuse or anger people. On the one hand, he stands by his truths. On the other hand, he is not stubborn about clinging to momentary impressions. Here is an illustrative example from his book *Love's Hidden Symmetry*:

> "Once, in a seminar of mine, there was a young woman—she was really nice, such a nice woman—and she had the urge to help men. She moved in with a man who had been married once and had two children. She was about 23 or 24 years old and the man was something like twelve years older than she. I told her, 'You have to leave him.'
>
> "A few months ago I get a letter from her saying that she was happily married to the man. She wrote, 'You were right. He wasn't the right man for me. I moved out and during the time we were separated, I noticed that I really do love him. Than I got back together with him and I really am happy.'
>
> "That's how it is with therapeutic recommendations. So much for my advice. They are right and final, but somewhat different in their effect."

What could be more confusing? What are we to think of a therapist's advice, when the client goes against it and is, in spite of this, doing the right thing? People want advice that they can act upon and orient themselves around. We seek universal, long-lasting truths. Could it be that he doesn't really want to commit, but that he just wants to put his finger to the wind? Does this practice of contradicting himself, which is further illustrated in the following excerpt of an interview, have a purpose?

> *Hellinger:* I have learned from many people, but I see the most in the current moment. So, if it is demanded of me, I expose the situation and the people in question, and above all, those that have been ignored. When I have all of them in view and I look to them with love and respect, the solution comes to me at once and then I say it. After a certain time, I recognize certain patterns.

> *Linz:* You gain experience from that.

> *Hellinger:* Yes, and from experience I recognize patterns which repeat themselves, such as the way that past partners of the parents are frequently represented in some way by the children.

> *(a short time later)*

> *Hellinger:* I always present the "truths" that I see in the moment and which anyone else can see when he pays attention to what's going on in the moment. For me, the truth is something that is shown to me in the moment and which reveals to me the direction for the next step. When I see something like that, I say it with full confidence and then I check it—according to the effect it has. If the same thing happens in another situation, I don't hearken back to the earlier image—after all, I'm not preaching a

gospel written in stone—but I look every time at what is going on in that moment. Although it may be different from what happened earlier—or even contradictory—I say it with the same sense of conviction, because what is happening during that moment does not allow for anything else.

Linz: So you don't make any hard and fast rules?

Hellinger: Absolutely not. On that same note, when one says to me that I said this or that two days ago, then I feel misunderstood, because he is implying that I wouldn't look at what is happening in the moment. I am always looking at something with fresh eyes, because one moment's truth is replaced by another moment's truth. That is why, to me, what I say is only valid in the moment that I say it. This focus on the truth of the moment is what I mean, by the way, when I call what I do "phenomenological psychotherapy."

Linz: But doesn't that contradict what you already said about the patterns?

Hellinger: Exactly. I face the contradiction when it arises and then weigh one side against the other.

What kind of truth is a truth that is only supposed to be true in a particular moment? We have heard from wise people and philosophers that the truth is a paradox and is composed of contradictions, but it rubs us the wrong way when we encounter it in every day life. "Either/or" is the principle that we orient ourselves towards, not "both/and." When someone contradicts himself, it is looked down upon and considered to be a sign of an intellectual or characterological weakness.

And when a person stands by his contradiction and does not even try to explain it, this is something that is as odd as it is infrequent.

That is why minds are divided on the subject of Hellinger and his work. What appears to one person as a deep, wise insight shocks another as groundless, unsubstantiated arrogance. Another thing he does causes tension among many, as well. On the one side, he stands completely behind his momentary insight, which is his own personal truth. On the other side, he does not require that another person see or have the same truth. From an interview with the magazine *Psychologie heute*, comes this excerpt:

> *Question:* When a person observes you doing your work, he notices that you often present people with very hard truths. When a contradiction arises and you provoke criticism from others, you then nip it in the bud by saying something like, "Then it isn't how I said it was."
>
> *Hellinger:* That way I avoid the discussion and controversy. If a person doesn't want to see something the way I see it, I have nothing against it. I don't want to defend my view. That is part of retreat. The main thing is that I can have my view and the other can have his.

The life accomplishments of Bert Hellinger are enormous. He single-handedly developed family constellations in their current form, based on the teachings of those who came before him. With that, he opened up an area previously unknown, which had been excluded and overlooked in most other therapeutic areas.

To me, Hellinger is like a pioneer who has made his way to a new continent in order to explore it. To do this, a person has to have particular qualities. Pioneers can't have a "well-rounded" personality; they need edges and a certain mixture of boldness and severity—towards themselves and towards others. A person who is nice, friendly and self-satisfied will not be able to see past his own plate.

Above all, a pioneer needs the ability to see something through to the end, to get things done and to "hang on"- a certain stubbornness and tenacity, in order to survive the endless trip across the ocean, without knowing if land is really there or if he will actually find it. Those who reach land and want to live on it will find many hurdles to overcome. He must be willing to fight, to get injured—and perhaps to injure others. To be fair to others at every turn, for a person on such a life path (just as on many other life paths), seems to me to be impossible.

In Hellinger's early years, a certain brusqueness, which could sometimes hurt others, seemed to be characteristic of him. It often caused him and his comments, to appear very harsh. He came across as rigid and unyielding, even merciless at times.

This harshness, which often seemed unnecessary, was not found to be an essential part of the work with family constellations. In the last few years, Hellinger himself has almost completely shed it. Instead of that sharpness, a certain gentleness has emerged—though he still possesses the inner power to be very direct and firm, when necessary in decisive moments.

Today, the love that stands behind him and his work becomes more and more noticeable. We, as people, sometimes have a very one-dimensional view of what is considered loving. One view of what is loving usually corresponds to something like a nurse who consoles the sick and dresses their wounds. But if the wound is badly infected, this type of love is not enough. Then a surgeon is needed, who takes a scalpel and makes an incision. Bert Hellinger is just such a lucid surgeon and he has the rare courage to sometimes cut like a knife—something that can at first shock an onlooker.

That which shocks people also attracts them. The hope and expectations that some people put on Bert Hellinger are enormous and thus unrealistic. The demand for him is huge.

My experiences with Hellinger at one of the three-day training classes with him in Freiburg were astounding. I organized the seminar for seriously ill clients, in front of an audience of people from the fields of psychology and psychiatry. Seven months before the event, all 650 seats had been sold. By the day of the seminar, I had to turn away nearly the same number. Ten months before the date of the seminar, I received the first of many inquiries from clients who were in the middle of a crisis and were hoping for a constellation with Bert Hellinger—ten months later! Although the seminar had been sold out, many people had traveled from afar in hopes of getting in anyway.

A kind of criminal energy, which is otherwise unusual in the community of psychotherapists, broke through. One man was caught with a counterfeit pass to the seminar. At the opening of the second day, one hour before the start of the seminar, aggressive vying for seats broke out.

In this way, Hellinger encountered expectations of healing which were blown out of proportion. It is apparent that Hellinger speaks truths that only pertain to the moment, and it is also apparent that people would like to hold on to his truths as gospel. His confidence and conviction make one feel at ease and he attracts followers. There are those, however, who simply quote Hellinger, instead of seeing or experiencing things for themselves.

Critical observers of the scene bring new terms to the developments as they see them. "Guru" is the first word. Ursula Nuber in an article in 1995 in *Psychologie heute* begs to differ:

> Hellinger says himself, that he is not a "guru." And unlike other psychological gurus, who populate the psychotherapy and above all the esoteric scene, he never had the intention of becoming a guru. He cannot help the fact that his fans and followers make him into a guru, because they very clearly have a strong need for authority and leadership. And exactly *that* is what is disconcerting about the phenomenon of Bert Hellinger.

Four years later, the same magazine arranged for a member of the evangelical headquarters in Berlin to write a piece on Hellinger, which then put him and his work in the same category as religious sects. It's my opinion that this could lead to such radio talk show themes as "The Family Constellation Therapy Fad: Wonder-Weapon in Family Conflicts or a Psycho-sect Scam?"

Here is another accurate description of the situation from a letter to the editor in a 1995 edition of *Psychologie heute*:

> This is my view on the "phenomenon of Bert Hellinger" as it can be seen from his biography. He forged his way through the entire jungle of therapy and did not get stuck in any specific type of it. Instead, he continued on his search for what works. It seems to me that Hellinger has become one of the few people who have found the inner independence to rely on his own opinion and trust it. A personal strength and authenticity grows from that independence, which people feel and are impressed by (and which is sorely lacking in many others).

There are different ways of reacting to him and his accomplishments. For example, I can (1) raise this man to the status of Guru, make statements taken from a special context as if they were written in stone and make him into a shepherd and myself into a sheep. Or, (2) I perceive this tendency among some and start to fight against this "guru" (such as we find in *Psychologie heute*). A third possibility—one which I prefer—would be to respectfully take in this man and his ideas, let myself be stirred up and effected by him, test his results for myself and then develop my own opinion.

To conclude my discussion on Hellinger, I will cite here a verbal exchange from one of Hellinger's seminars.

Hellinger: A master was never a student and a student will never be a master. Do you know why? The master sees and that is why he doesn't need to study. The student learns and that's why he doesn't see.

Participant: That's a joke.

Hellinger: That is what the fool says.

Participant: What you just said contradicts many schools of spiritual thought.

Hellinger: That doesn't concern me.

Participant: I didn't say that it should concern you; I said that it is a contradiction of many schools of thought.

Hellinger: I am aware of that. But when you take a look at the students, you see that many are a disgrace to the master.

Traditional therapists and those who set up family constellations are separated into two camps against each other. "Bert Hellinger and Systemic Psychotherapy: Two Different

Worlds," from Simon and Retzer is the title of one of the few written commentaries on family constellations. There have been very few analyses of family constellations so far and due to its relative newness it's no wonder. The science and practice of psychotherapy needs time to work on those things which were previously unknown and they are not in any hurry. That's why there is little knowledge of family constellations in many circles. Usually the psychotherapeutic community comes into contact with family constellations only when workshops or presentations are given at conventions. Often, the reaction there is a vague rejection.

One of the biggest concerns of those in systemic family therapy, who have substantially different views from Hellinger, is that others will confuse their systemic work with that of Hellinger's. Since the demand for Bert Hellinger is so strong, the danger exists (in Germany at least), that the average person will always think of Bert Hellinger when they hear the word "systemic." That, according to the article mentioned above, is already giving the systemic therapists pause. After all, a person who mentions the name Hellinger and the word "systemic" in one breath is making a false (narrow) claim.

That's why "Bert Hellinger's Systemic Psychotherapy" is often rejected by those who wish to claim a monopoly on the word "systemic" and also why attempts are made to forbid Bert Hellinger from using it. But two points are salient here: to try to own a word like "systemic" for one's own use, does not seem reasonable, and, perhaps most importantly, Hellinger himself makes no claim to a unique brand of "systemic therapy."

Which reservations against family constellations are truly substantial and what are their foundations? One objection is aimed at the "orders" in families and relationships that were developed by Bert Hellinger and described herein. Aren't such orders just a fabrication resulting from a conservative and outdated worldview? Is Hellinger just claiming his ideology as truth and making it his teaching? And is he able to sell this teaching based solely on the power of his personality, "healing" clients who are just easily influenced? Is he just espousing "biblical family orders and patriarchally-based structures" for today's over-taxed population who might then regress, as the critic Heiko Ernst suspects?

One thing that surprises me in regards to the criticism is the phenomenon of the critics overlooking the fundamentally new discovery in family constellations. This is the discovery of the "Knowing Field" and the connection that the representatives have with it. Hellinger—and every other family constellation facilitator—lets himself be guided by the reactions of the representatives, as well as the clients. In this way, family constellations also can be seen as a type of research instrument. During the constellation, the representatives react spontaneously with the feelings that belong to that respective role, feelings which are often very clear. The principles and orders are, after all, just a way to guide us. There are many variations and exceptions that are taken into consideration. Only after something serves to satisfy something in the system, only when all of those taking part feel accepted and in good hands within the network of the relationships, can one attempt to put the representatives into a more beneficial order. Family constellations take the uniqueness of each family very seriously.

Many critics of this work must have a blind spot which prevents them from perceiving the "Knowing Field" that is made visible through the representatives' feelings. Only in this way could they claim that Hellinger alone directs and instructs the whole process. Simon and Retzer voice that view in this way: "It is Hellinger's portrayal of the family— which is his own subjective view—which has been made a basis of therapeutic intervention. But Bert Hellinger claims that the participant sets up the family as he or she sees it or experienced it."

Only a person who had never actually experienced a family constellation and the influence that the representatives have on it could write this. Such a perspective reveals a person who has so filtered his perceptions, that the new and previously unknown phenomenon that constellations has introduced, have escaped his notice entirely. To critique Hellinger's work according to such criteria is only possible when a person overlooks certain decisive points.

Aside from that, critics attribute a conservative ideology behind his work and then accuse Hellinger of this. The term "conservative" has thus become an indictment of him. Family constellations are about concepts like family, bonds and guilt. Surely the archaic language that Hellinger uses (which remind one of his past as a priest and missionary) also contribute to that.

To a certain degree, the critics are right to say that the orders found in constellations contradict some modern, "progressive" ideas and ideologies. Concepts like ties and responsibility disturb a person who dreams of freedom and choice without limits. The deciding question is not whether the orders that Hellinger observed in the constellations are "conservative" or "progressive." A more appropriate question is, Are these orders effective or not? If the answer is yes, then they affect us much more than we are aware, whether we agree with them ideologically or not.

Hellinger did not develop his views on orders abstractly or theoretically. They emerged, rather, from the practical therapeutic work with clients setting up family constellations. The principles and orders were not prescribed, but rather learned about and discovered through practical observation. Anyone can rediscover them for himself in a constellation. In a constellation, they are testable, because they must be used by different therapists, in constellations of a wide variety of topics, yet still lead to a solution.

In addition, Hellinger does not preach about any "ideal" nuclear family. According to my own observations, it is the so–called "ideal" family that can be the most problematic, because life and the living are destroyed by the "morals" that control the actions of the "perfect family". The practice of excluding the "black sheep," for instance, exists routinely in such a family. Some people in such families take on the view that they are better than others and have more of a right to live and to belong to the family. It is this superiority that is the worst transgression against the family order, and sometimes the hardest to uncover. The problems in "dysfunctional" families, however, are much easier to solve in the constellations, as they are much more apparent.

It is the bond with the family that hinders a person's development. The way through life begins with this bond and later, when a person finds the order within the family and acknowledges these orders and bonds, people become free. Then the bond with the family becomes a source of strength rather than a burden and you can go even one step beyond, which is to bond with something greater.

One legitimate point of criticism seems to me to be the belief by some family constellation facilitators, that a constellation is a panacea of sorts. For example, a woman had spent twenty years going through every type of therapy possible in order to rid herself of a problem. The problem is resolved though a family constellation. Excitement and triumph boil over among some in the psychological community. People start to believe that with family constellations, any emotional problem can be healed within minutes.

This brings us to the issue of disappointments and setbacks in family constellations, which have not often been addressed. This is also due to the relative infancy of constellations as a type of therapy. It is no wonder, that people who have no experience with family constellations often react skeptically and rightfully so. The best source of information is one's own experience. Now that family constellations are slowly coming of age, these topics are waiting to be studied. Family constellation facilitators are now beginning to address this topic: "Mystification of family constellation? A plea against promising too much" (Gloeckner).

There is no well-balanced assessment of the outcome and possibilities of this work, nor of its limits. On the one hand, constellations can open new doors and allow people deep insights within a short time. That is something that can shock some people and cause others to put up defenses or resistance. For example, a person who believes that psychoanalysis of several years duration is necessary for such deep insights, would naturally be mistrusting of the results of a constellation that took place in the course of an hour.

The explosion of family constellation facilitators in Germany also came as a shock to colleagues in other areas of psychology. The demand for family constellations in Germany is enormous and therapists from other schools have noticed it. In addition, family constellations complement and support other types of therapy, which can lead to briefer therapy. Perhaps what we find with many critics is—and this is entirely human and thus understandable—that they are worried about the future of their "turf", income or livelihood.

What should we think about warnings of dangerous constellations and facilitators? The range of education and experience of facilitators who claim to work in the style of Bert Hellinger is wide. It includes on one hand, professionally trained and educated psychotherapists—experienced psychiatrists and psychologists—and on the other, personal coaches and armchair psychologists. Recently, for example, a well-intentioned minister's wife told me of family constellations that she carried out at her church, after completing one weekend training seminar with Bert Hellinger.

Without a doubt, the number of constellation facilitators is growing at a very fast pace. It is enough for some to be fascinated with the work in order to believe they can do it. Theoretically, anyone could claim that they facilitate "family constellations according to Bert Hellinger". There is no copyright. A certain amount of wariness of the untrained, inexperienced facilitator who is trying to be a "little Hellinger" seems to be justified.

When a new type of therapy develops, the normal course of things is—after a short beginning phase—for someone to try to create a monopoly on the service and to defend such actions. First the name of the method becomes reserved and then institutes are founded—the best way being to found only one true institute. Training in the method is developed and offered. The training starts out shorter in the beginning, with longer and longer courses offered over time. There are practicals, tests and finally "graduates" who have the right—according to a diploma or certificate—to facilitate the method.

Bert Hellinger holds a different view of such things. He doesn't see himself as the "inventor" of family constellations—someone who must now defend his rights like the owner of a patent. Instead, he feels that he is the person through whom family constellations came into the world, without him wanting anything from it or making any claim to them. His view is that he discovered something that any other person is equally capable of seeing.

To me, it is crazy for a person to try to pocket a reality that can be seen by anyone. It pains me when someone asks me if she is allowed to use something that I have said or done—as if I had rights reserved on certain realities or insights. They came as gifts to me and are there for everyone else as well! If someone sees them and passes them along, I have no claim to them. I have been inspired, I pass this inspiration on and it pleases me when others pass it on in the same way.

Bert Hellinger has an unusual amount of trust in family constellations and in the people who want to perform them. A therapist who wants to go down this path starts at the beginning, as is customary, just as every cow starts out as a calf. One does not need to be perfect, but rather a person decides to start out. The path leads further and further and in time, greater challenges and more severe problems come and you expose yourself to them. What Hellinger does emphasize, is the importance of the therapist knowing his or her limitations.

Who should you go to and on whom can you rely when you want do a family constellation? In this jungle of family constellation facilitators, is there anything like "quality assurance?" At present, the only type of quality assurance is word of mouth recommendation. Gunthard Weber founded the association "Systemic Solutions According to Bert Hellinger" (Systemische Loesungen nach Bert Hellinger—see appendix). This association looks for ways to let constellations develop and grow freely while at the same time building a certain framework of safety and credibility.

In the first edition of the association's magazine, "Praxis der Systemaufstellung" (The Practice of Setting up Systems), the mission-statement read, "The spread and further development of phenomenological, systemic procedures, which is above all tied to the practice of family constellations. To spread it in a respectful way and to have an effect in an informed, integrated way on the development of this movement."

They recommend as a prerequisite for setting up family constellations, that those who want to work with this approach have a basic education in psychotherapy and/or social work and a few years of experience seeing clients. In their opinion, the approach of Bert Hellinger is not a stand-alone therapy. According to the association, Hellinger's method can be best learned through experience and direct observation. They further believe that it is important for those who want to use this type of therapy in groups, to do the following:

- set up their own family of origin and current family constellations in a group led by an experienced therapist or facilitator who has learned the work in seminars with Bert Hellinger.

- get experience in setting up their own family as well as observing other families in several family constellation seminars led by experienced colleagues.

- take part in a supervision group as they begin to work on their own.

A person who wishes to set up his own family in a family constellation is responsible for finding a qualified family constellation facilitator. He should first learn something about the facilitator and his or her background. He might talk with others who have experience with the facilitator. The client can then make an informed decision about whether a facilitator is best for him.

Personal Experiences from Family Constellation Participants

Scientific research on family constellations is in the beginning stages. At this point, little information and almost no statistical data about its effectiveness can be given. There is more and more anecdotal information available, however, as time goes on.

I found two thesis papers which are important because they interview clients about the issues for which they sought out family constellations and later ask about the effects of the constellation and their level of satisfaction with the outcome. I, myself, sent a questionnaire to 90 people who had done constellations on their own families. The questionnaire asked them about the results of their constellation. Almost half of the people queried, responded and these results were the same as those found in the theses.

Dorothea Rieger made available to me her psychology thesis, which was a study that she and Inge Stueckmann of Freiburg, Germany, conducted. They questioned 39 people who had taken part in family constellation seminars, each led by one of four different facilitators.

The most consistently positive result of the thesis was the answer to the question about whether or not that participant would recommend attendance at a family constellation seminar to a friend. Thirty-seven of the thirty-nine answered the question with a "yes," and two with a "no." Here are some reasons given by those who answered in the affirmative:

> "The most important thing for me is that this method is based upon love and respect, that it connects us to our families in a very positive way and that it reawakens love and brings it into motion."

> "It brings clarity to the family history."

> "Although I did not respond wholeheartedly to my constellation, I learned a lot from other people's constellations and the dynamic principles at work really touched me."

> "It is a very good way of uncovering hidden problems in a short time."

The other questions varied more. In spite of the general recommendation that people would give, there were different levels of satisfaction. Of the 39 people, 31 said they were satisfied, 6 were partially satisfied and partially unsatisfied and one person was unsatisfied.

These results show that family constellations often do not completely fulfill the expectations that the participants have built up. The expectations are especially high when people set up their own family. However, that which is missing in one's own constellation is often made up for in someone else's.

The participants came with a host of issues to the seminars and several people had two or three issues. The issues ranged from existential themes to concrete relationship problems. Here are some examples:

"I'm afraid of not being held."

"I want to find out the truth about my family."

"I want to be able to have a relationship and closeness with someone."

"I would like to have more peace and trust."

"I'd like to find out why I always want out of the relationship."

"I want to understand why my oldest daughter is unhappy."

"I'd like to improve my relationship with my oldest son.

Three months later, a follow-up questionnaire, about any changes experienced, was sent out. Seven issues had been completely resolved, 36 issues had experienced various degrees of improvement, fifteen issues remained unchanged and one issue had worsened.

These results could be interpreted as being positive as a whole, though not all wishes were fulfilled (which, by the way, is an unrealistic expectation). These results agree with my own experience, to the point that I believe that additional, more extensive examination of the effects of family constellations would confirm these findings.

In the thesis from Guido Junge of Hamburg, Germany, just seven clients were asked about their experiences in family constellations in open, semi-structured interviews. Their constellations had taken place six months to three years prior to the interview.

The solutions found in the family constellations were accepted by all of those interviewed and described by them as being effective. Every client's image of their family had changed in some way, their place in the family had changed and their attitudes towards other family members had also changed. The constellations were predominantly experienced as "freeing" or as a "release" which for most was a huge relief. Some of the clients had been in therapy for several years and experienced this method as a valuable compliment to previous therapy. These feelings are expressed in the following testimonials:

> "One thing that I notice very clearly, is that my relationship to my mother has really changed. . . . I am now able to accept her the way she is and I no longer need to focus on how she treats me. And I also no longer have this feeling that I have to *do* something. For 33 or 43 years, I had this feeling that I want to be somewhere else and that I'm not getting there. Now I see that it doesn't have to be that way. It's okay."

> "I don't see my family so often any more. I used to see them fairly often. . . . Last summer was the first time that I didn't have any desire to stay with them more than a few days. . . . They live their life and I live mine. I've sort of allowed myself to have that. And the more I allow myself to have that, the easier it is for me to be with people or to reach out to them.

> "Something in that relationship (to the mother) has fundamentally changed. I am able to do both—love her but at the same time refuse some of her wishes, if I don't want to do it. And she was okay with that."

> "My feelings for my siblings are much, much stronger. That happened already after my first constellation. They are very important to me. On the outside, I don't have any more contact with them, but I have noticed how important they are and how much they are a part of me and in my heart, and that it is good that they are there."

"Things are getting better with my son. He said that I have become stricter. I don't think that that is so much the case as that I used to be very unclear and wishy-washy with him. I have become much clearer about what I want from him, which has also brought me somewhat closer to my daughter."

"After the constellation, I became more at peace with my husband. I drove home and thought to myself, 'it's okay now.' I didn't talk with him about it, but it had an effect on him and things are moving along well. I am still standing by my decision to go ahead with the divorce. But I no longer have to be so angry with him."

"The time just after my family constellation was anything but a resolution of our family problems. It was a very emotional time. Deep inside, I had that image of my family found at the end of the constellation and I knew how it could feel. On the outside, though, I often found myself in the role of an observer. Indeed, I was observing myself and how I relate to my family. It was a long time before I had the feeling of being satisfied with my position in the family. On the road to this satisfaction, there were many arguments and crises, which did end up leading to a resolution." (Guido Junge himself)

NINE

What Can I Do By Myself?
Researching the Family History.

At the completion of this book, not every reader will immediately want to set up his own family in a family constellation seminar. Sometimes, just reading the experiences shared by others from their constellations can be enlightening and bring some resolution. The many videos of Bert Hellinger facilitating family constellations get even more under one's skin. The atmosphere in the videos is palpable.

With knowledge about the orders and connections in families, curiosity is aroused. Suddenly, the family history isn't just old stories forced on us by a grandmother or an aunt. The old family photographs that had been gathering dust in the closet become more alive and we see them with new eyes.

A participant in one of my seminars told me at the beginning of the seminar, "Just answering the questions that you sent before the seminar was worth the cost of the seminar. For the first time ever, I talked with my parents about our family's past. I learned so many new things—things which we had never talked about before."

A person who researches his family history can get some surprising insights. It is helpful to find the answers to the following questions (in regards to the family of origin):

- How did the parents get to know each other?

- How old were they at the time?

- How old were they when they got married?

- If they didn't get married or if they later separated or got divorced, what was the reason?

- Did the mother have important past loves, fiancés or husbands?

- Did the father have important past loves, fiancés or wives?

- How many siblings do you have (including half-brothers or sisters)?

- How many siblings does your mother have?

- How many siblings does your father have?

An early death in the family is often one of the most important causes of entanglements:

- Do you have siblings who died young?. (younger than thirty; stillbirths count as well.)

- Did your father or mother die when you were younger than age fifteen?

- Did any of your siblings have a special "fate?" (Examples of special fates can be found below.)

- Did your mother have any siblings who died young?

- Did your father have any siblings who died young?

- Were there any siblings on the maternal grandparents' side who died young?

- Were there any siblings on the paternal grandparents' side who died young?

- Was there anyone in the family who had a child younger than fifteen years old die?

- Did any woman in the family die in childbirth, from the consequences of childbirth or did she sustain any injury in childbirth?

Crimes, gross injustices and guilt as a consequence of actions, have an effect on the family over several generations:

- Was there any family member who committed murder (or manslaughter)?

- Did any member of the family commit sexual abuse?

- Was anyone involved in war crimes? In what way?

- Was anyone cheated out of an inheritance or did they inherit something unjustly?

Special fates in the family have to do with someone being shut out of the family, harsh personal fates or loss of the biological parents or the homeland:

- Was there anyone in the family who committed suicide?

- Was anyone the victim of a crime?

- Was there anyone who was mentally or physically handicapped?

- Did anyone spend time under psychiatric care or in a psychiatric facility?

- Did anyone spend time in prison?

- Did anyone in the family go bankrupt?

- Was anyone homosexual?

- Was anyone shut out of the family in any other way, for any other reason (alcoholism, gambling, etc)?

- Did anyone emigrate?

- Were there children born out of wedlock?

- Was a child given up to foster parents or relatives?

- Was anyone adopted?

- Was anyone driven from his homeland; did anyone flee from his homeland?

- Does anyone have parents of two nationalities?

- Was there any other type of tragic fate?

- Do similar fates exist somewhere in the mother's or father's family?

- Do similar fates exist somewhere in the grandparents' families?

- Do similar fates exist somewhere in the great-grandparents' families?

Finally, it is worth finding out about those things in the family that would rather be kept secret. It usually has something to do with a crime or it is something embarrassing, having to do with sexuality:

- Are there family secrets?

Note: It is not appropriate to ask one's parent's about abortions in their relationship, but abortions in other generations may be known about, though kept secret.

Drawing a family tree gives one a good overview of the family. Information about each member can be written in by their name on the diagram.

Finally, there are many ways of creating a family constellation in your own imagination. With all of the actions I propose below, it is important to pay attention to your own reaction to them and to take your reaction seriously. Ask yourself, What happens in me when I do this? Do any of these things touch me in some way? Do any of these imagined actions anger me. Do I feel any resistance? Do any of these make me feel good?

When imagining each action, it is helpful to close your eyes and take enough time, so that the person in question has clearly emerged in your imagination. Speak the proposed sentences calmly and without emotion.

Imagine your mother and/or your father and say to them, "I place myself next to you."

Imagine yourself bowing with respect to your mother or father and then say to them, "I honor you and your fate."

Imagine your mother and/or your father and say to him or her, "I am like you." And/or, "I do things like you do."

Imagine your mother and/or father and say, "I help carry the burden—out of love."

Imagine your mother and father beside each other and say to them, "What is between you two has nothing to do with me. I am just the child and I don't have to choose between you. I have you both."

Imagine your mother or your father behind you, holding you.

Imagine your mother and/or your father in front of you and say, "I take what you have given me and I thank you for it. It is a lot and it is enough. I can do the rest myself."

What is it like for you to imagine yourself deeply and strongly connected to your family and to your father and mother in particular?

Imagine a family member who has been excluded from the family and say to him or her, "I belong with you." (You can also say, "You belong to our family.")

Imagine a former partner of yours and say to him or her, "Thank you for what I received from you. You may gladly keep what you received from me. I take my part of the responsibility for what went wrong in our relationship and I leave your part with you. I give you a place in my heart as my former partner. (And if there are children, "Through our children, we remain connected, as mother and father.")

Imagine a place on the "other side," where all of the deceased in the family are lying. Go there and lie with them. Lie there at peace with them for a while. When it's enough, stand up again and come back to the light.

BIBLIOGRAPHY

Andreas, Connirae: Core Transformation: Reaching the Wellspring Within. Real People Press, Utah 1994.

Baitinger, Heidi: "Ist nach dem Familien-Stellen eine Nacharbeit notwendig?" Weber, 1998.

Barth, Rüdiger: "An die Grenzen, bis es weh tut." *Zeitung zum Sonntag*, 8.3.1998

Brink, Otto: "Familien-Stellen mit Schuhen," *Weber*, 1998.

Douglas, Kirk: Interview in *Stern*, Volume 37/98.

Ernst, Heiko: "Biblische Psychohygene," *Psychologie heute*, 6/1995.

Franke, Ursula: "Stellen Sie sich vor, Sie stehen vor Ihrem Vater und schauen ihn an—Systemische Interventionen in der Imagination," *Weber*, 1999.

Franke-Griksch, Marianne: "Systemisches Denken und Handeln in der Schule," *Weber*, 1999.

Franke-Griksch, Marianne: "Vom Paar zur Familie—wenn sich ein Kind ankündigt. Systemische Arbeit und Familien-Stellen mit schangeren Paaren," in Weber 1998.

Glöckner, Angelika: "Mystifizierung des Familien-Stellens? Ein Pladoyer wider die überzogene Verheisung," in *Praxis der Systemaufstellung*, Volume 2/1998.

Goleman, Daniel: *Emotional Intelligence*, New York: Bantam Books, 1995.

Grolle, Johann: "Es gibt kein Halten mehr," Spiegel, 48/1998.

Hellinger, Bert: Wo Demut heilt und Ohnmacht Frieden stiftet, Heidelberg 1998.

Hellinger, Bert: Interview with Marion Rausch, not published.

Hering/Rössner: Tater-Öpfer-Ausgleich im allgemeinen Strafrecht, Bonn1993.

Ingwersen, Dagmar und Friedrich: "Erfahrungen mit dem Familien-Stellen in einer psychosomatischen Rehabilitationsklinik," *Weber*, 1998.

Junge, Guido: "Familienaufstellung nach Bert Hellinger. Eine qualitative Untersuchung anhand einer Nachbefragung von Klienten," a doctoral thesis in psychology at the University of Hamburg, 1998.

Junior, Boia Efraime: "Wer weinte, mußte sterben," special edition *50 Jahre Stern*, 51/97.

Krober, Prof, chair of the institute of forensic psychology of the University of Hamburg, interview, *Stern*, 51/97.

Leicht, Robert: "Warum Walser irrt," *Die Zeit*, 3.12.1998.

Leutz, Grete Anna: Das klassische *Psychodrama nach J. L. Moreno*, Berlin, Heidelberg, New York 1974.

Liedtke, Susanne: "Die Würde der Zellmasse," in Spiegel Special, 1/1999.

Mahr, Albrecht: "Anne Ancelin Schützenbergers transgenerationale Psychotherapie," Praxis der Systemaufstellung, Heft 2/1998.

Mahr, Albrecht: "Die Weisheit kommt nicht zu den Faulen. Vom Geführtwerde und von der Technik in Familienaufstellungen," in Weber 1998.

Mai, Karl-Georg, psychiatries and therapist at the department of forensic psychiatry in Prison Institutions (*** Maßregelvollzugs), Stern, fifteen/98.

Milz/von Kibe'd (Hg.): Körpererfahrungen, Anregungen zur Selbsterfahrung, Zurich 1998.

Nuber, Ursula: "Eine unheimliche Ordnung," *Psychologie heute*, 6/1989.

Pigani, Erik: "Nos aieux se melent de notre destin. Psychogénéalogie: Comment se liberer du cycle des répétitions familiales," *Psychologies*, 1/1989.

Scheucher/Szyszkowitz: "Systemische Aufstellung zum Bosnienkonflikt. Krieg im Nachbarland—was braucht der Friede?" *Weber*, 1998.

Schneider, Jakob: "Familienaufstellungen mit Einzelklienten mit Hilfe von Figuren," *Weber*, 1998.

Schützenberger, Anne Ancelin: *Aie, mes Aieux, Desclée de Brouwer*, Paris, 2nd Edition, 1998.

Schützenberger, Anne Ancelin: "Health and Death: Hidden Links through the Family Tree," *Caduceus*, issue 35.

Sheldrake, Rupert: *Seven Experiments that Could Change the World*. New York: Riverhead Books, 1995.

Simon/Retzer: "Bert Hellinger und die systemische Psychotherapie: Zwei Welten," in *Psychologie heute*, 7/1998.

Sparrer, Insa/von Kibe'd, Matthias: "Wie Systeme Systeme wahrnehmen. Körperliche Selbstwahrnehmungen bei systemischen Strukturaufstellungen," in Milz/von Kibe'd.

Villeneuve, Jacques: Interview, *Spiegel*, 22/1997.

Weber, Gunthard (Hg.): Praxis des Familien-Stellens. Beiträge zu systemische Lösungen nach Bert Hellinger, Heidelberg 1998.

Weber, Gunthard (Hg.): *Praxis der Organisationsaufstellungen*, Heidelberg 1999.

Weber, Gunthard und Gross, Brigitte: *Organisationsaufstellungen*, Heidelberg 1998.

Recommended Reading on Family Constellations and Addresses for Further Information

Hellinger, Bert; Weber, Gunthard; Beaumont, Hunter; *Love's Hidden Symmetry*. What Makes Love Work in Relationships. 1998 ISBN 1-891944-002, Zeig, Tucker & Theisen, Inc.

Hellinger, Bert; ten Hovel, Gabriele; Acknowledging What Is. Conversations with Bert Hellinger. 1999. ISBN 1-891944-32-0, Zeig, Tucker & Theisen, Inc.

Neuhauser, Johannes (ed.), *Supporting Love*. Bert Hellinger's Work with Couples. 2001. Zeig, Tucker & Theisen, Inc.

Systemic Solutions Bulletin, a biannual publication printed in England. Inquire with Barbara Morgan, e-mail: Barbara@stotfold89.freeserve.co.uk

Dr. Bertold Ulsamer
Runzstr. 48
D-79ten2 Freiburg,
Germany
Tel.: 49-761-706418
Fax: 49-761-706456
http://www.ulsamer.com

Bert Hellinger's website: http://www.hellinger.com
http://www.hellingerschule.com

Information on Family Constellations in areas outside of Germany can be found at:
www.constellationflow.com (Australia)
www.constellationsolutions.co.uk (Great Britain)
www.systemicfamilysolutions.com (United States)

Dr. Bertold Ulsamer, Ph.D., holds degrees in law and psychology. As a psychotherapist, he specialized in NLP (Neuro-Linguistic Programming) and was a management consultant in that field for fifteen years. Since 1995, he has led family constellation seminars, and has carried out continuing education seminars on the subject in Europe, Asia and the United States. He is the author of seven books on the topics of communication and self-management and he is one of the editors of *Praxis der Systemaufstellung*, a journal of Bert Hellinger's work. Dr. Ulsamer and his wife Gabriele live in Freiburg, Germany.

Dr. Ulsamer's other texts on constellation work:

Spielregeln des Familienlebens. Anregungen nach dem Ansatz von Bert Hellinger. (written with Gabriele Ulsamer) Herder, Freiburg, 2000

The Art und Practice of Family Constellation. Leading Family Constellations as Developed by Bert Hellinger, Carl-Auer-Systeme-Verlag, Heielberg 2003 (German version: Das Handwerk des Familien-Stellens. Eine Einführung in die Praxis der systemischen Hellinger-Therapie, Goldmann, München 2001).

Mit der Seele gehen. Interview with Bert Hellinger, (with Harald Hohnen), Herder, Freiburg 2001.

Wie hilft Familien-Stellen? (Martin Hell) Vier-Türme-Verlag, Münsterschwarzach 2003.

Spielregeln für Paare. Einsichten in Partnerschafts-dynamik mit dem Familien-Stellen nach Bert Hellinger, Goldmann, München 2003.

Zum Helfen geboren? Antworten für hilflose Helfer aus dem Familien-Stellen, Vier-Türme-Verlag, Münsterschwarzach 2004.